T0194413

COMMON SENSE -
A Real Party Movement

JAMES WEART,
JURIS DOCTOR

COMMON SENSE - A REAL PARTY MOVEMENT

iUniverse books may be ordered through booksellers or by contacting:

iUniverse
1663 Liberty Drive
Bloomington, IN 47403
www.iuniverse.com
844-349-9409

Because of the dynamic nature of the Internet, any web addresses or
links contained in this book may have changed since publication and
may no longer be valid. The views expressed in this work are solely those
of the author and do not necessarily reflect the views of the publisher,
and the publisher hereby disclaims any responsibility for them.

Any people depicted in stock imagery provided by Getty Images are
models, and such images are being used for illustrative purposes only.
Certain stock imagery © Getty Images.

ISBN: 978-1-6632-1024-1 (sc)
ISBN: 978-1-6632-1023-4 (e)

Library of Congress Control Number: 2020919463

Print information available on the last page.

iUniverse rev. date: 10/14/2020

PREFACE

IN ORDER TO UNDERSTAND WHERE the country is today, it is important that you understand the History of the American Colonies, of the Political Parties of the United States and of the United States of America. I will attempt to tie the three together in order to assist you in coming to a common sense conclusion that the Democratic Party and Republican Party have outlived their political usefulness.

HISTORY OF THE AMERICAN COLONIES

ON OCTOBER 12, 1492, CHRISTOPHER Columbus landed on San Salvador and planted the Spanish Flag. During the 1500's a race to claim new lands and riches developed between Spain and Portugal. Spain obtained most of South America, all of Central America, Mexico, and parts of modern-day California, Arizona, New Mexico, Texas, and Florida. Portugal, being smaller and less powerful, managed to take control of a large portion of land in the central portion of South America (modern day Brazil) and numerous small islands in the Southern Hemisphere.

Meanwhile, the other European powers, England, France, and Holland sat idly watching as the Spanish and Portuguese gained wealth and power from their conquests in the New World. The English, aroused by the defeat of the powerful Spanish Armada in 1588, struck first establishing a colony in Jamestown, Virginia, in 1607, and in Plymouth, Massachusetts

1

in 1620. Soon thousands of English settlers set sail for the new continent of North America landing up and down the Atlantic coast from Massachusetts to Georgia. Not all of them were coming for land and riches, as many were escaping religious persecution and the iron fisted rule of the King and his Nobles. There was a longing for religious and personal freedom they could not enjoy in England.

The French also got into the act establishing a military fort near modern day Jacksonville, Florida, to keep the Spanish from moving North from St. Augustine, Florida, which they had settled in 1565. While France did claim a few small islands in the Caribbean, their main land holdings would be in the area of Quebec, Canada, and the huge territory called Louisiana that stretched from New Orleans up the Mississippi River to present day Southern Minnesota. It was a huge land mass but was only densely populated by the French in the New Orleans area. The rest of it was very sparsely populated.

The Dutch sent settlers into New York, Pennsylvania, and New Jersey. They were also able to lay claim to several islands in the Caribbean Sea and some land in northern South America, but overall finished last in the race for the New World.

The big losers in the above land grabs by the European powers were the Indians, or present-day Native Americans. They were lied to, cheated, swindled out of their lands, and slaughtered without mercy if they resisted. Their pristine natural habitats were destroyed, crops, pillaged, and large herds of game ruthlessly hunted by the European settlers. They were forced from the natural lands of their ancestors and made to move away to unknown destinations to escape the hordes from Europe.

The English eventually established thirteen colonies under their control: Massachusetts, New Hampshire, Rhode Island, Connecticut, New York, New Jersey, Pennsylvania, Maryland, Delaware, Virginia, North Carolina, South Carolina, and Georgia. For a while things went fairly well but disputes over commerce, land, representation, taxation, and incompetent British governors appointed by the Crown eventually led to discontent with the government in London. By the mid 1700's, the French to the north (Canada) and west (Louisiana Territory) were creating problems for the colonists. They made treaties with various Indian Tribes and encouraged them to attack English settlers in areas the French were claiming such as western Pennsylvania, the Ohio River Valley, and parts of Western North Carolina (modern day Tennessee). The British, in kind, attacked French settlements in Quebec and along the St. Lawrence River in order to exploit their naval superiority over the French. A series of small wars followed culminating in the French and Indian War of 1753, until 1758, during which a young Virginia Militia Officer named George Washington rose to prominence. His experiences in fighting the French and Indians around Fort Duquesne (near Pittsburgh) and eventually commanding 1500 militia men to guard a 400-mile front from Maryland to North Carolina made him a well-known military tactician to the Colonists. After the war he returned to his life in Virginia as a plantation owner.

In 1763, the Treaty of Paris required the French to relinquish all their territories in Canada and claims to Western parts of the colonies to the British. France would make no more claims to English territory in North America after signing the treaty. However, the French and Indian War would be one of the major factors which caused the Revolutionary War against the British. King George III of England had fritted away his predecessor, King George II's, full treasury on frivolous ventures and schemes thrust upon him by unscrupulous members of the Royal Court. Since his royal treasury had dwindled down to nothing, he decided to tax the Americans heavily using the excuse that the French and Indian War had drained the English treasury. The Americans knew that the King was lying, as they had contributed the majority of the troops in the war on the side of the English and helped supply the soldiers with the necessities of war. So, when Parliament levied a series of taxes on the American Colonies at the Kings insistence, the Colonists were infuriated. Soon discontent and acts of civil disobedience spread throughout the colonies with Massachusetts leading the charge. The laws imposed duties on imported glass, paper, tea, lead, paint, sugar, rum and certain manufactured goods. Worse yet, the Quartering Acts required private homes to provide billeting facilities for British soldiers stationed in the Colonies. No one took kindly to British soldiers living in their homes. Finally, in 1770, a large mob demonstrating in the streets of Boston started taunting and throwing snow balls at a squad of British soldiers. Someone yelled "Fire!" and the Redcoats opened up on the mob. Several people were killed and numerous others wounded in what would become known as militias with adequate stores of rifles, munitions, and supplies needed for war.

In April, 1775, the British marched out of Boston headed towards Lexington and Concord to seize rebel leaders Sam Adams and John Hancock, as well as stores of muskets, munitions, and supplies hidden in those towns. The Colonists were forewarned by Paul Revere that the Redcoats were coming and about 70 militia men were waiting for them in Lexington. A British Officer rode forward and ordered them to disperse and lay down their arms. The Minutemen Commander told his men not to fire unless fired upon, but if the British wanted a war to let it begin there. Sure enough, someone got trigger happy and a shot rang out followed by a huge volley from the British troops. The minutemen being heavily outnumbered and outgunned dispersed. The British moved on to Concord where a much larger and better trained militia force was waiting. In the ensuing battle the British took heavy losses and eventually retreated back to Boston, while subjected to constant ambushes from patriots shooting at them from behind walls, fences, trees, barns, and farmhouses. This was not the "European Gentlemen's" type warfare to which the British army was accustomed. This militia mob had just inflicted losses of 273 men dead or wounded on the world's greatest army while only losing 93 of their own. As one dejected British Politician put it: "Whoever looked upon the American colonists as an irregular mob will find himself much mistaken." The American Revolution had begun.

Soon, Patriots from the other colonies came to Boston's defense and George Washington arrived at the invitation of Congress to lead them. By January of 1776, he had established the First Continental Army which promptly surrounded Boston and placed 69 cannons and mortars seized from the British on Dorchester Heights pointed at the city. The British, vastly outnumbered, their supply lines cut, and their ships vulnerable to the rebel cannons, wisely requested to withdraw from Boston, if Washington would allow safe passage. Washington reluctantly agreed and on March 17, 1776, General Howe and his army sailed for Halifax, Canada. The Americans triumphantly entered Boston to wild cheers from the local population.

On July 4, 1776, the Continental Congress ratified the Declaration of Independence and declared the American Colonies, "Free and Independent States" forever severing ties to the English Crown. General Howe was forced to act by King George III and soon attacked Washington's army, which was fortified in Brooklyn Heights in order to defend New York City. A smaller American force was also on Long Island and in August of 1776 was routed by General Howe's troops who then outflanked Washington's army in Brooklyn causing them to slip back to Manhattan under the cover of darkness and fog on August 29th. Washington subsequently retreated to New Jersey, and the British occupied all of New York City. The British had avenged their earlier loss of Boston. However, this war to bring the American colonies back under British control was not going to be the short and easy one they envisioned.

After a series of attacks and reverses resulting in the British seizing Princeton, Trenton, Savannah, and large amounts of territory in the mid-Atlantic and Southern States, Washington surprised and totally routed a British-Hessian force on Christmas day 1776, at Trenton, New Jersey. A week later he defeated a large reinforcement column outside of Princeton and went into winter quarters around Morristown. The British no longer controlled New Jersey.

Alarmed by Washington's successes, General Howe left

New York and sailed up the Chesapeake Bay, ultimately seizing the rebel capital, Philadelphia. He simultaneously ordered General Burgoyne to march his army out of Canada and head south to New York City. The plan was to split the colonies and catch the Continental Army between these two larger British forces and finally destroy it. Washington received news of Burgoyne's southerly movement and dispatched Generals Gates and Arnold to stop him. The British having to march through rough terrain and facing engagements by colonial militia slowed to a crawl. It took them from July to October, 1777, to move 150 miles to Saratoga, New York, which was only halfway to New York City. By the time Burgoyne's army got to Freeman's Farm, just outside of Saratoga, General Gates was waiting for him. The British moved off to the south and on October 7, 1777, the combined forces of Generals Gates and Arnold decisively defeated them at Bemis Heights. Ten days later, unable to get reinforcements or supplies from General Howe, who was still in Pennsylvania, General Gates surrendered his entire force. This was the news Benjamin Franklin, who was in Paris seeking French aid in our revolution, needed to hear. He went to the Royal Court and persuaded the King of France to enter the war on the side of the Americans, which the French did in June, 1778. The remainder of the Continental army camped at Valley Forge during the winter of 1777-1778. Short of food and supplies, it was the worst of times for our army. Only the arrival of Boron von Steuben, a Prussian Officer with incredible training skills and disciplinary methods saved the army from collapse. His programs paid off when the Continental Army attacked a larger British Force under General Clinton at Monmouth Court House, New Jersey, in June of 1778. Although historians called the battle a "draw," the British took heavier casualties, lost more of their supplies, and eventually broke off the engagement in their haste to reach New York City. The Continental Army held their lines and made an orderly withdraw to West Point, New York, wherein Washington encamped for the winter.

He placed General Benedict Arnold, the hero of the British defeat at Bemis Heights resulting in Burgoyne's surrender at Saratoga in charge of the defenses of the fortress at West Point. Unbeknownst to George Washington one of his best generals had become disillusioned with his treatment by Congress and other generals in the Continental Army, and at the urging of his wife had agreed to turn the fort over to the new British

Commander, General Clinton, for a price. His treason was discovered only several days prior to the British attempting to acquire West Point when Major Andre, the messenger between Arnold and General Clinton, was captured with an incriminating letter detailing the plan to surrender the fort. Andre was hanged as a spy while Arnold escaped and joined the British Army as a Brigadier General.

In the Southern Colonies, British General Clinton was wreaking havoc on the Colonists, first taking Savannah and then Charleston. Most organized resistance was broken save some guerilla units under Francis Marion in South Carolina who were having success and disrupting British supply lines. General Gates was sent to North Carolina to rally the continental troops back into the fight but was severely beaten by General Cornwallis's British Army and fled the battle on horseback leaving his troops in disarray. Nathanael Greene was put in charge of what was left of the army in the South and soon had organized an effective guerilla fighting force that harassed Cornwallis everywhere he went. At Kings Mountain a detachment of Cornwallis's cavalry was butchered by patriot guerillas. Next, the British suffered a crushing defeat at the

Battle of the Cowpens in South Carolina. In 1781, after an indecisive battle at Guilford Court House in North Carolina, Cornwallis headed north to Virginia while Greene headed for South Carolina. Cornwallis counting on British naval superiority went to Yorktown, Virginia, where he fortified his position until the British Navy could extricate him. Unfortunately, he misjudged the French Naval and land forces, who had recently arrived to aid the colonists.

Washington made it appear to the British Commander Clinton that he was going to attack New York City with the aid of the French Fleet. This caused the British to further fortify New York and the British Fleet to remain there. Meanwhile, Washington marched his army south to Yorktown along with a large contingent of French soldiers. The French Fleet coordinated with Washington and sailed into the Chesapeake Bay to cut off Cornwallis escape by sea. By this time, the British saw what was happening and dispatched ships to rescue Cornwallis. In a fast-moving sea battle, the French Fleet managed to out sail and outshoot the British Fleet which sailed back to New York for repairs after a humiliating defeat. 8,000 British and Hessian soldiers were now surrounded and pounded daily by American and French cannons by land and the French Fleet by sea. It was only a matter of time before Cornwallis' men ran out of food, water, ammunition, and other necessities for waging war. On October 19, 1781, it was all over. Cornwallis surrendered to Washington and 8,000 British troops laid down their weapons before the victorious Continental and French Armies. Back in London King George III and parliament were stunned. How could this group of ragged, undisciplined, underequipped, and undersupplied colonists have beaten the greatest army in the world? Maybe it was that they were fighting for freedom and the right to govern themselves, whereas the British were fighting for power and wealth. The war did not officially end until 1783 when the Treaty of Paris recognized the sovereign new nation of the United States of America and ended all claims by Great Britain to any of her territory. The U.S. was granted significant western territory from the existing colonies to the Mississippi River.

CREATING A NEW NATION

JOHN ADAMS, HIS COUSIN SAMUEL Adams, and John Hancock, all of Boston, had started the revolution in 1775, which had ended with a new independent nation. The next step was to figure out how to set up a government that would embody all the principles laid out in the Declaration of Independence and still be fairly administered to all of the thirteen new states, regardless of their size and population. This created a unique challenge for the Congressional delegates when they convened in 1787 in Philadelphia.

The formula for the original constitution was to create three distinct branches of the government: The Executive Branch would be the President, Vice President, and cabinet members; The Legislative Branch would be the Senate and House of Representatives; and the Judicial Branch would be the Supreme Court of the United States and the Federal District Courts at the trial level. Each Branch would have their own specific powers and duties to perform and each would be a check and balance against the other two, so no one Branch would reign supreme. It was an ingenious system that allowed the President to lead the country, while the Legislative Branch passed laws that moved the country forward, and the Supreme Court interpreted those laws when challenged in court, and ruled on legality of the President's and Congress' actions when questioned. Each Branch could reel another one in if the offending Branch were overstepping its constitutionally mandated powers. The problem was that the original constitution forgot to spell out the constitutional rights of the common citizen. In 1791, Congress corrected this deficiency by passing the first 10 Amendments to the United States Constitution, commonly known as the "Bill of Rights."

These well planned and composed
Amendments are as follows:

First Amendment-

Congress shall make no law respecting an establishment of religion, or prohibiting the free exercise thereof; or abridging the freedom of speech, or of the press, or the right of the people peaceably to assemble, and to petition the Government for a redress of grievances.

This covers several rights at the same time. Freedom of Religion means you have the right to worship a Supreme Being or God as you see fit according to your religious beliefs. It does not, however, allow you to assault or kill someone in the name of your God because that person does not believe the same way you do. Freedom of Speech or of the Press means what it says – you have the right to say what you want and the Press to report what they want as long as it does not incite or cause illegal or adverse consequences. For example, a person falsely yelling "Fire" in a crowded restaurant for the thrill of watching everyone run for the door and trample each other is not free speech. Likewise, a television reporter falsely saying that a large meteor is headed for a named city in order to cause panic and chaos, resulting in numerous deaths or injuries as people attempt to flee the city is not free press. It also gives people the right to peaceably assemble and address their grievances to the Government. It does not give them the right to set businesses on fire and loot stores as we have recently seen in the Black Lives Matter Protest Marches, as it allows the people to "peaceably assemble."

Second Amendment –

A well-regulated militia, being necessary to the security of a free State, the right of the people to keep and bear Arms, shall not be infringed.

Our most controversial Amendment means what is says. It does not say that if some lunatic shoots up a school, a night club, a church, or a concert, that 100 million law abiding gun owners must give up their guns. Apparently, some people who have not read their history books and who do not understand that our constitutional framers knew exactly what they were doing want to repeal this Amendment. Adolph Hitler and Joseph Stalin would greatly approve of that because an unarmed population can have a democratic republic internally overthrown by a group of armed fascists, or communists, or terrorists. Likewise, it makes a foreign invaders job much easier in taking over the country when no one has guns or ammunition to oppose them. You need to look at the causes of these mass shootings. You see, the guns do not decide to get out of their gun cases and walk to school and start shooting. Kids who have been bullied over and over by their classmates via the internet are the ones who finally snap and seek revenge on those who have taunted and degraded them. Or the kid who is receiving terrorist propaganda via the internet and thinks it would be really cool to go shoot up a synagogue to impress his new internet friends from the Middle East. How about the X-box games that all the kids are playing? You know the ones where the guy is shooting up everyone he sees, and brains and guts are splattering everywhere, and no one can stop him because he's a cool super killer. Wow, I'll bet you that's never inspired any of these kids to go shoot up their school. No, it's the guns. I've heard them talking in their cases or boxes saying please come take me somewhere so I can shoot people. Yeah, it's not all the violence in the movies and games, or the terrorists' propaganda and bullying on the internet, it's those talkative guns with little feet that causes it all. I'll tell you what people – when you give up your internet, cell phones, violent movies and games, and stop your kids from bullying each other to the point of causing kids to commit suicide and shoot up schools, I'll give up my guns. Do we have a deal? Certainly not, because you do not want to give up what is really causing these shootings... electronic internet and amusement devices.

Third Amendment –

No soldier shall in time of peace be quartered in any house, without the consent of the owner; nor in time of war, but in a manner to be prescribed by law.

This amendment was passed because prior to and during the Revolutionary War the British required the Colonists to allow at least two or more soldiers (depending on the size of the house) to be quartered in the colonist's residence. Can you imagine having two Chinese, North Korean, or Iranian Soldiers staying at your house? Hey, maybe that Second Amendment is not looking so bad after all.

Fourth Amendment –

The right of the people to be secure in their persons, houses, papers, and effects, against unreasonable searches and seizures, shall not be violated and no warrant shall issue, but upon probable cause, supported by Oath or Affirmation, and particularly describing the place to be searched and the persons or things to be seized.

This is the most litigated Amendment of all. I have probably argued this Amendment and its State counterpart a thousand times in court. The key is that the warrant has to be supported by enough sworn facts to give the Judge probable cause to believe that evidence of a crime will be found at the place of the search or the person to be seized has committed a crime. The British would send their soldiers into someone's house or business and search it and tear up its contents on a suspicion or hunch that someone might be plotting against them and their King. They did not need reliable facts to establish probable cause for the search because they were not required to have a warrant to search your house and therefore your socialist-communist advocates would argue the government's right to search outweighs the individual's right to privacy so why should they have to get a warrant? Not to mention your new Chinese, North Korean, or Iranian friends who are already living in your house and obviously don't need a warrant to search it. Hey, maybe that Second Amendment is starting to look a whole lot better.

Fifth Amendment –

No person shall be held to answer for a Capital, or otherwise infamous crime, unless on a presentment or indictment of a Grand Jury, except in cases arising in the land or naval forces, or in the militia, when in actual service in time or War or public danger; nor shall any person be subject for the same offence to be twice put in jeopardy of life or limb; nor shall be compelled in any criminal case to be a witness against himself; nor be deprived of life, liberty, or property, without due process of law; nor shall private property be taken for public use without just compensation.

This is probably the second most litigated Amendment in court. The main focus of the litigation is the voluntariness of a defendant's confession. All too often, you hear of a person who admitted to a crime under duress from sharp police interrogators and then ten years later it is shown that he did not commit the crime. Of course, at the time this amendment was passed, it was a reaction to the British policy of beating a confession out of a Colonist or jailing him without bond until he confessed. The Double Jeopardy Clause prohibits the government from prosecuting you twice for the same offense. However, it does not prohibit your State government from convicting you of a crime, and then the Federal government from convicting you of the same crime. The Clause regarding your right to remain silent says you do not have to answer questions which might incriminate you while in police custody and cannot be required to testify during your trial against yourself. The British practice of requiring a Colonist to testify in court to prove his innocence then using his testimony to convict him strongly influenced the wording of this amendment. The Due Process of Law Clause has been liberally interpreted by the Courts and requires a trial wherein the accused' rights are strictly guarded. This was in response to the British practice of bringing an accused before a magistrate and convicting him on little or no evidence – trial by accusation and hearsay. The last clause allows citizens to litigate a government seizure of their property in Eminent Domain proceedings wherein the jury can determine the value of the private property taken for government purposes. Those Chinese, North Korean, and Iranian soldiers who are hanging out with you in your house will happily torture a confession from you for a crime you did not commit, or summarily find you guilty without a trial, or confiscate your property without paying for it. Hey, are you ready to give up your computers, cell phones, X-boxes, Video Games, and Violent Movies for my guns yet?

Sixth Amendment –

In all criminal prosecutions, the accused shall enjoy the right to a speedy and public trial, by an impartial jury of the State and District wherein the crime shall have been committed; which District shall have been previously ascertained by law, and to be informed of the nature and cause of the accusation; to be confronted with the witnesses against him; to have compulsory process for obtaining witnesses in his favor; and to have the assistance of counsel for his defense.

Another well worded Amendment in retaliation to the British practice if bringing someone before a magistrate and convicting them on hearsay evidence or letting the Defendant rot in jail without a trial until he confessed and pleaded guilty. The right to a speedy and public trial before a Jury with the assistance of counsel and being able to confront the witness against you is paramount to due process of law. Of course, try quoting this Amendment to those Chinese, North Korean or Iranian guys who have occupied your house and see if they give you a fair trial. Hey, are you having second thoughts about repealing the Second Amendment?

Seventh Amendment –

In suits at common law, where the value in controversy shall exceed twenty dollars, the right of trial by jury shall be preserved, and no fact tried by a jury shall be otherwise reexamined in any court of the United States, than according to the rules of common law.

This Amendment allows for a Jury Trial in civil cases and states that the Jury's findings of fact cannot be overturned or reexamined by the Courts. That is why the Appellate Courts will not overturn or reexamine the Jury's findings of fact unless they are clearly erroneous as not being based on the evidence presented in Court. The $20.00 limitation clause is not really practical anymore as I have never met a civil lawyer who's going to try a case before a Jury where the amount in controversy is $20.00. Maybe for Two Million they might.

Eighth Amendment –

Excessive bail shall not be required, nor excessive fines imposed, nor cruel and unusual punishments inflicted.

This Amendment is the one that the Defense Lawyers who specialize in Death Penalty cases always cite when challenging the method of executing a Defendant as "cruel and unusual." I never had a client catch it. However, since the Delegates to the Constitutional Convention who enacted this Amendment never defined the word "Excessive" (remember they thought $20.00 was a lot of money in Amendment 7), I have seen my share of outrageously excessive bail amounts set by Judges in drug trafficking cases. I'm sure the men who wrote this Amendment in 1791 would have agreed with me that a Million Dollar Bail in a Drug Trafficking case was clearly excessive. When I made that argument, the Judge must have forgotten his hearing aid as my argument fell on deaf ears. The main reason for this Amendment was to stop the former British practice of whipping people in public or making people stand with their head and arms in wooden stockades for days on end while passerby's could throw whatever they wanted at them. The British had by this time moved on to hanging or the firing squad as methods of execution instead of the old, cruel methods of drawing and quartering a man or disemboweling him like in the movie "Braveheart." However, foreign invaders such as your new Chinese, North Korean, and Iranian roommates might prefer the old cruel and unusual methods. Are you still upset with Amendment 2?

Ninth Amendment -

The enumeration in the Constitution of certain rights shall not be construed to deny or disparage others retained by the people.

This is primarily not used very much in court. It appears to be an escape clause that says if your State gave you more Constitutional rights then the Federal Constitution did then that's ok with Congress.

Tenth Amendment –

The powers not delegated to the United States by the Constitution, nor prohibited by it to the States, are reserved to the States respectively, or to the people.

Forget the Courtroom on this Amendment. The 10th Amendment is the only one that went to "Trial by Combat" and cost over 600,000 lives. It was decided in such places as Manassas, Antietam, Fredericksburg, Gettysburg, Vicksburg, Chickamauga, Atlanta, Petersburg, The Wilderness, and Appomattox Court House. The Framers of the Constitution had realized in 1791 that all the 13 States wanted a limited central government with the majority of the legal powers being retained by the individual States within their own borders. This is known as the "States Rights Doctrine" and was embodied in the language of the Tenth Amendment. The South seized on the language of the 10th Amendment in 1861 saying "the powers not delegated to the United States by the Constitution... are reserved to the States, respectively." The South's argument was that the Central Government of the United States located in Washington, D.C., had been given limited specific powers by the Constitution such as the coining of money, the raising of an army and navy for defense from foreign aggression, certain limited taxing authority, regulation of commerce between the States, establishing a National Bank, building certain government buildings for the Executive, Legislative, and Judicial Branches of government, and other limited powers.

Nowhere, the South argued was the Central Government given such authority as to dictate to the people of (for example) South Carolina and Virginia how to live every facet of their daily lives.

Slavery was one of the issues that caused the war, but there were numerous other disagreements between the Northern and Southern politicians regarding taxation of goods going to and from Europe, the majority of which came out of the South. When the matter came to a boiling point, South Carolina was the first State to withdraw or succeed from the union. Ten other States, including Virginia followed her out of the Union. In April, 1861, Confederate gunners fired hundreds of cannon balls into Fort Sumter, South Carolina. The "Civil War," or the "War Between the States," or the "War for Southern Independence" had begun. It would rage for four years until April, 1865, when the Confederate States of America surrendered and ceased to exist. The country was reunited under a strong central government

Americans that the movement seems to be attempting to change history by attacking all monuments, flags, and references to the Confederate States of America. Are we going to delete April, 1861, to April, 1865, from the history books?

These 10 Amendments to the U.S. Constitution should not be amended or repealed as the men who wrote them had more wisdom and knowledge than any of today's politicians.

When George Washington was sworn in at the First President in 1789, the three Branches of government were untried and had to grope about in the dark to find their way. By the time, his administration was over in 1797, it appeared all three Branches were seeing the light and clearly understood what was required of them. Our democracy had gotten off the ground and was slowly moving forward. There had been serious doubters as to whether it would last through Washington's eight-year administration. By sheer determination, hard work, and intelligent compromises the Founding Fathers made our government strong at a time when most countries in the world were still ruled by Kings, Queens, and Nobles. This Democracy idea was working.

After Washington left office, there would be a series of good presidents – John Adams, Thomas Jefferson, James Madison, James Monroe, and John Quincy Adams in office moving the country forward economically and militarily. During Madison's administration we had a second war with the British from 1812 to 1815 with the same result wherein Andrew Jackson emerged as a popular war hero. By 1829, the former army officer, lawyer, and Senator would become President despite his controversial past and rough demeanor. He was not born of the landed, rich gently like his predecessors but came from poor stock. However, by the time he became President, he was one of the largest landholders in the State of Tennessee, who still held the rich in disdain. He was so strong willed and decisive that his political enemies referred to him as a King. Because he was from the western part of the country (as it existed in 1829) he was looked upon with skepticism by the political powers of the east. He was the first President elected solely by the popular vote, instead of the back room deals previously worked out in the Electoral College. In his case, the Electoral College votes actually mirrored the popular vote to the shock of the political establishment. There were many in politics at this time who felt that the American people were really not smart enough to rule themselves and the democracy experiment was not working. Why should not the rich, powerful, and wiser men rule since these uneducated peasants did not understand the working of government? (Sound familiar?) Despite his lack of social graces, Andrew Jackson proved them wrong. By the end of his presidency in 1837, everyone knew that a common man who came up through the ranks could make a good president. More importantly, he had taken the fledgling Democratic Party from a non-powerful faction to the strongest political party in the United States.

By 1845, we were involved in a war with Mexico during the administration of President James Polk, who had served under Andrew Jackson and been an excellent student of Jackson's dog eat dog political style. By the time the war was over in 1848, the United States had acquired Arizona, New Mexico, California, and the war had allowed Texas to finally be annexed as a State. Furthermore, President Polk had negotiated a deal with the British that required them to renounce any claims to the modern states of Oregon and Washington. He had acquired a vast area in the west which eventually would add to the tension between the North and the South over slavery.

By 1854, the Whig Party and remnants of the old Democratic Republican Party formed a new party opposed to the expansion of slavery and to the Democratic Party of Andrew Jackson's followers and called it the Republican Party. Thus began the greatest political rivalry in the history of the United States with the election of Abraham Lincoln in 1860, followed by the Civil War, and continuing until the present. To say that the rivalry between the supporters of Hillary Clinton and Donald Trump in the election of 2016 has brought us to the brink of another Civil War would not be an understatement. The hatred expressed between Democrats and Republicans of today is at about the same level as it was in 1860, just before the Southern States succeeded. By April of 1861, the South fired the first shots upon Fort Sumter and the war begun. Both sides thought that it would be a quick affair, lasting maybe two months with light casualties on both sides and a negotiated truce. Little did they know that it would be the most destructive, murderous, and costly war in lives and property that Americans would ever fight. It lasted over four years with over 600,000 dead and countless wounded. The lack of decent medical care during the war resulted in hundreds of thousands of amputees, as the quick solution to an arm or leg wound was to cut it off. After the war, the States were burdened with huge financial debts in order to care for the wounded veterans. The ill effects of the war were to last over 100 years.

Since the North won the war, they were able to write its history the way they wanted. For example, they called it the "Civil War" while the Southerners called it the "War for Southern Independence." A civil war means both factions and seeking to take over the entire control of the nation. The South argued that they were merely trying to break away from the control of the North and had no aspirations to rule the Northern States – thus no "Civil War." They just wanted to be left alone.

The Northerners have always said that the main reason the war was fought was over slavery. That was one of the reasons, but not the primary one. The primary reason was the loss of tax revenues to the United States government if it let eleven Southern States and two Territories slip away. Prior to the war of the South exported huge quantities of cotton, tobacco, sugar, indigo, and other agricultural crops to Europe, Canada, and South America. These products generated huge tax revenues for the U.S. Treasury because of the tariffs on the outgoing crops and on the incoming manufactured goods that foreign countries sent back to the Southern States. The North was so industrialized, it did not have to import manufactured goods from foreign countries at the rate the South did. Thus by 1860, the South was providing over 60% of the national tariff revenues to the U.S. Treasury. This was a huge sum of money that the North could not let go. Also, the South had an abundance of natural resources such as timber, precious metals, furs, water sources, and fertile soil for agriculture, that were worth far too much money to give away. The real proof is that nine out of ten Southern whites did not own slaves. They could not afford them. The average white family in the South made between $35.00 to $45.00 per month in 1860. The average price for a black slave field hand was between $1,000.00 to $1,800.00 depending on the location of the slave market.

It is obvious then that the only people in the South who could afford to buy slaves and feed, shelter, and maintain them were the filthy rich plantation owners. So, the average soldier in the Confederate Army was not fighting for the institution of slavery but was fighting for the right of each individual state to be free from a central government controlled by people of different cultural beliefs. Since the population of the North greatly outnumbered the Southern population, they had complete control of Congress and could literally dictate the law to the South. Realizing that the original Colonists who settled the South in the 1600's were from Scotland, Wales, and Northern Ireland, whereas the people who settled in the North were from England, Holland, France, and Scandinavia, the cultural differences should be apparent. A British observer who had travelled extensively throughout both the North and South said that the South succeeded from the North because the two are not homogeneous as they have different instincts, appetites, morals, and cultures. Having spent time in Virginia, Florida, and Georgia, on one hand, and New York, New Jersey, and Rhode Island on the other during the 1950's, 1960's, and 1970's, I can tell you beyond a shadow of doubt that they were two entirely different worlds one hundred years after the Civil War. So, I cannot imagine how incredibly different they must have been in 1860. Maybe as different as Tennessee and California are today.

Quite frankly, if the Civil War had only been about slavery it would have been totally unnecessary as slavery would have died an economic death by the mid 1880's. Advances in farm machinery powered by steam, diesel, or gas engines would have killed it. Why spend all the money required to buy, feed, house, and maintain numerous slaves when you can buy one machine for $15,000.00 that will do the work of 100 slaves? Southern plantation owners looking at the cost of maintaining the slave force would have let them go as being cost ineffective. Sort of like the car industry today – why employ a human on the assembly line when a robot is so much more cost effective?

Am I justifying slavery? Of course not. I am only pointing out that it was a necessary evil in the plantation system until the advent of something better. And remember – the Northern shipbuilders and industrialists benefited from it as well. The guilt of slavery must be borne by the entire country – not just the South. The Southern Soldiers were fighting on their own terrain, had better generals, had grown up hunting, and therefore had the advantage. However, the North, being heavily industrialized, could out produce the South in cannons, rifles, ammunition, naval vessels, uniforms, boots, foodstuffs, and supplies needed by an army. It was just a matter of time. Put a naval blockade around the South, keep attacking on all fronts, and eventually you will wear them down and bleed them out. Destroy their infrastructure and their ability to resupply their troops like General Sherman did in Georgia and South Carolina and they will be unable to continue to fight. Keep coming at them over and over again regardless of the losses as General Grant did at Vicksburg and on the Virginia peninsula and eventually their lines will break. Grant was the only Union General who understood that you could never outmaneuver or outfight General Robert E. Lee of the Army of Northern Virginia. You had to outlast him and take bad beatings before you could overwhelm him. Other Union generals never figured that out and would retreat and lick their wounds after Lee beat them in battle giving him valuable time to resupply and move his army to a more strategic location. Grant just kept coming at him never giving him the time that he needed. The North lost many battles but still managed to win the war. Sometimes it's better to slowly and methodically strangle your enemy as General Grant proved.

Several days after General Lee surrendered to General Grant at Appomattox Court House, Virginia, President Abraham Lincoln was shot dead at Ford's Theatre in Washington, D.C. by

John Wilkes Booth, an actor and Southern sympathizer. While Booth thought he was doing the South a favor, the opposite was true. Lincoln had planned to go easy on the South and assimilate it back into the United States without being too harsh on them. After his death, the Northern Republican controlled Congress put such economic and punitive measures on the South that 100 years later it still had not recovered. South Carolina went from being one of the wealthiest States in the country in 1860 to being one of the poorest after the war. Lincoln's successor, Andrew Johnson, being from the South, could not stem the tide of anti-southern sentiment that permeated the country. The North was treating the South like a conquered land at the same time Northern Cities were passing ordinances which discriminated against newly freed Southern Blacks, who were moving North in hopes of a better life. The war had not had very many positive accomplishments except for the profiteers supplying the military, smugglers running the blockade, and embalmers and undertakers around the country. There was hardly a household anywhere in the country untouched by the death and destruction of the war. Nothing was settled by it as the "freed" slaves still were not really free and a lot of great issues that could have been resolved never were. The nation was still divided in 1865. It still is today but for different reasons.

A series of wars against foreign powers would temporarily reunite the country. The War of 1898 with Spain, World War I, and World War II united us against enemy nations. Certainly, by the end of World War II having defeated the powerful totalitarian military machines of Germany, Italy, and Japan, the United States emerged as the strongest and most powerful nation on earth. In September 1945, our country was the most united, it had been since George Washington was inaugurated as our first President on April 30, 1789. At that time our entire country was united under his presidency as the nation finally had a government for the people. Washington <u>warned against</u> establishing political parties with party platforms that sought to obstruct the execution of laws already created, or to prevent certain branches of the government from enacting the powers provided to them by the Constitution. (Sound familiar?) While the nation was completely united at that time, a few years later the John Adams (Federalist) vs. Thomas Jefferson (Democratic Republican) political party fight would start the great divide that Washington warned against. Only War World II would of well-equipped Chinese soldiers along with incredibly cold conditions causing our mechanized divisions to falter resulted in the North Korean – Chinese forces taking back the North Korean territory we held. Finally, a stalemate ensued, and both sides signed an armistice where the North – South dividing line was where it had been in 1950. Nothing had been gained by either side except the United States had approximately 40,000 military personnel killed. While there are no totally accurate figures of enemy combatant losses, the estimates based on eyewitness accounts and other data are the Chinese Army lost 400,000 dead and the North Korean Army lost 100,000 dead. The good news was we were told by the government that we had stopped the spread of Communism, which unfortunately would soon be on its way to Vietnam.

The French had begun colonizing the Southern part of Vietnam in 1859 and by 1887 had control of all of Vietnam, Laos, and Cambodia. They kept control of this area until 1940 when they were persuaded by the German Nazi Army, who had occupied France after defeating its army, to allow Germany's ally, Japan, to occupy large parts of Vietnam in the North along the Chinese border in order to stop the flow of arms from the

Western powers to China. At the time China was fighting the Japanese. The combination of French and Japanese soldiers occupying Vietnam was more than nationalist leader Ho Chi Minh could stand. He organized the Viet – Minh in 1941 to free Vietnam from foreign rule. By 1945, the Japanese had to leave Vietnam after losing in World War II. The French were no longer in the commanding position they had been in prior to World War II. Ho Chi unleashed a communist backed guerilla movement and by 1954 had inflicted military defeats on the French resulting in a peace treaty wherein his Communist government was given the Northern half of Vietnam while its Southern half would be ruled by an independent government with ties to France and the United States. The French military would be required to leave. Then new elections were to be held by 1956 in order to vote on reunification of the country and the election of the leaders. These elections were never held at the insistence of the United States who argued that the North Vietnamese guerillas who had infiltrated the South would force people to note for Ho Chi Minh and therefore the election would be invalid.

Right after the defeat of the French, Ngo Pinh Diem

arrived in South Vietnam from Europe as the newly appointed Prime Minister of the country. Diem had come from a noble Vietnamese family with ties to the French government and was Roman Catholic. He had previously served as the Vietnamese' Emperors Minister of the Interior but relinquished his title and stepped down from public life due to a dispute with the French rulers of the country. In 1945, he was captured by Ho Chi Minh's troops. Ho tried to persuade him to join the communist cause but Diem refused and went to Europe to await further developments. In 1954, the Vietnamese Emperor Bao Dai asked Diem to come to South Vietnam as its Prime Minister. The following year Diem ousted Bao Dai and declared himself President of South Vietnam. He became a dictator surrounding himself with relatives and close friends in the government and ruled with an iron fist. He initially had the full support and backing of the United States due to his anti-communist stance. Soon he had communist backed insurgents, the VietCong, attacking his government. His persecution of the Buddhist majority and favoritism of the Catholic minority led to riots and demonstrations against his government. Finally, in November of 1963, the top generals in the South Vietnamese Army launched to be a colony of the United States like they were to France. However, it appeared his top generals wanted the United States to send more combat troops and supplies into their country. Likewise, President Kennedy felt that having 15,000 advisors to assist the South Vietnam Army and sending supplies and weapons of war to them was help enough. He would never have approved of having 540,000 American soldiers, sailors, airmen, and marines sent to Vietnam. Yet, by 1969 that is how many Americans were there. The Military Industrial Complex wanted to escalate the war to a much larger scale. President Kennedy would not do it. However, they learned that Vice-President Lyndon B. Johnson would be willing to send as many troops as needed to South Vietnam. So, the same C.I.A. that backed the overthrow and killing of President Diem of South Vietnam is the same C.I.A. that helped Lee Harvey Oswalt assassinate President Kennedy. Oswalt was shown to have communist leanings, to have lived in Russia, and was a former marine who was an excellent shot. He also was not very bright and could be easily manipulated by a C.I.A. operative posing as his friend, so he was the perfect "Patsy" who would have appeared to act alone. The proof of the motive were the facts

facts in order to get you, the average citizen, to do their bidding. How many young 19 year old draftees knew why they were in Vietnam? How many of them knew who was on their side versus who was the enemy? How many of them knew what the overall strategy was to win the war, because their commanding generals sure as hell did not. How many times were they required to capture key enemy positions, only to have to abandon those positions the next day, at which time enemy forces would retake the position without having to fire a shot. To make matters worse, these poor draftees who were serving their country with honor and courage were hearing horror stories about protestors back home calling them baby killers and war mongers. There were no parades for them when they got home, unlike the World War II Veterans who got a hero's welcome. To the contrary, they were spit at and disparaged by protestors who did not know, understand, or appreciate what they had done. It is much easier to fight a war when the whole country is behind you, than it is to fight an undeclared war where the majority of the country is against you. The Vietnam veterans are true heroes.

The moral of this story is never get in the middle of a

foreign country's civil war because it is a lose – lose situation. As Ho Chi Minh said to an American reporter – "We've been here for thousands of years. You just got here. How long are you willing to fight us because we can outlast you?" And that is exactly what they did. They did not beat us militarily, they just turned the tide of public opinion back home against us, waited it out, and watched us quit and go home. Then they took Saigon from the ARVN.

The real Party of America, a third party I am proposing will have a platform that we are not fighting for foreign countries that will not fight for themselves. We are not the world's policemen to right the wrongs of the world. We need to put our money back into the infrastructure of the United States and stop throwing trillions of dollars into the Middle East to help people who hate us solve their internal power struggles. If you know your history, you will know that the people of the Middle East have been slaughtering each other for the last 12,000 years. But we Americans are going to change all that in a few short years. Really? They are tribal in nature and have blood feuds that go back thousands of years, but we are going to stop it all. It's not about the people – it's about the oil under those deserts. The government is telling you our military is there to help those people. Actually, they are there to protect our oil interests. Wake up to the truth.

Afghanistan is a different story than the Iraq, Kuwait, and Syria debacle. We needed to destroy the Taliban and their training camps after the 911 attacks on the World Trade Center and the Pentagon. We pretty well accomplished those feats in the first two years we were there (2001 to 2003) in that we had destroyed the training sites, disbursed the Taliban and installed a friendly government in power. So, do we leave around late 2003 or early 2004? Of course not. We stay there until the present for no apparent reason other than to show the world that we can. Real Party of America Policy – Get the hell out. Enough is enough. We did not adopt these people to raise. They need to raise themselves.

Same thing with the Iraq, Kuwait, Syria scenario. Get out.

Where then should we stay, you ask. South Korea comes to mind due to the unstable nature of its neighbor to the North. Possibly a small group of military advisors to remain in Germany and Japan. Otherwise, send everyone home who is stationed overseas. We cannot afford in lives and dollars this military expansion our government has thrown on us. It is the something the Romans did, and it caused their downfall. Will not that weaken our military position you ask? Only if you ask our troops to fight a war with no clear objective and no clear strategy to win. If you have a clear objective and allow our military to fight without stupid rules, we can win in a hurry. War requires an absolute ability to unleash hell on earth on your enemies to the point they will beg you to stop. These ridiculous tactics of trying to make best friends out of your enemies, showing mercy and compression, have no place in war. Case in point – taking all those ISIS prisoners in Northern Syria and allowing them to escape will cause huge problems in the future. They should not have been taken prisoners to begin with. Their prior atrocious and murderous conduct, a well as their terrorist status, should have called for their summary execution. The troubles in the Middle East will never end. So, if you want to solve them all you will need to do is have U.S. Troops there for thousands of years into the future, and, of course, drain our treasury dry. That, my fellow Americans, is the future of the Middle East and our future if we stay there.

Why cannot Egypt, Israel, Saudi Arabia, Kuwait, Quatar, Lebanon, and Jordan form an alliance to help defend each other from ISIS, Taliban, and Iranian aggression since they all seem friendly to the Western Powers? Why do we have to do it? We should not have to, and we will not.

HISTORY OF POLITICAL PARTIES IN THE UNITED STATES

IN 1787, WHEN CONGRESS RATIFIED the United States Constitution setting up our current form of government, there were no real organized political parties. By the time it took effect in 1789, George Washington was the nation's first president and several prominent men were advocating the formation of political parties in order to campaign for the presidential election once Washington's term of office was over. Despite the fact that President Washington felt that organized political parties were counterproductive fearing conflict and stagnation, Alexander Hamilton and John Adams were champions of the Federalist Party while James Madison and Thomas Jefferson formed an opposition party known as the Democratic – Republican Party. The Federalists wanted a strong central government with close ties to Great Britain, a central banking system, and close interaction between the central government and men of wealth and power. In effect, they were the elitist party who by sheer status wanted to rule the rest of the country in a manner similar to that of the former rule of the British. The Democratic – Republicans strongly opposed the Federalists agenda wanting to reserve most of the power to the individual states and keep the new central government from assuming too much power. John Adams, an original member of the Federalist Party, was the second President of the United States from 1797 to 1801, when Thomas Jefferson of the Democratic – Republican Party became the Third President for the next eight years. By 1828, the Federalist Party was dead and the Democratic – Republican Party had spilt into the Democratic Party led by Andrew Jackson, the Seventh President of the United States from 1829 to 1837, and the Whig Party led by Henry Clay. The Democrats wanted strong presidential powers which outweighed any other branches of government whereas the Whigs wanted the Legislative Branch to have more power than the President as to keep him in check. The two parties fought over many other issues, most notably a central banking system run by the government, taxation, protective tariffs, regulation of industry and commerce and the evil of slavery. By 1854, the Whig Party was nearly dead as a prominent Anti-Slavery during his term of office from 1913 to 1921, leading us through World War I and the Peace Treaty thereafter. President Herbert Hoover was blamed for the economic chaos which brought on the Great Depression of the 1930's. President Franklin D. Roosevelt, a Democrat, emerged as a hero who saved the country from the Great Depression with his New Deal, as well as leading it successfully through World War II. Post World War II, a great General and Republican, Dwight Eisenhower, served as President from 1953 to 1961. Upon the expiration of his presidential term, this former Supreme allied Commander of all forces in Europe during the Second World War made a prophetic speech where he warned us to "Beware of the Military – Industrial Complex." Four years later in 1965, President Lyndon Johnson, a Democrat, sent a large contingent of U.S. Marines to a far-off land that no one heard of: Vietnam, in order to quell a Communist backed Civil War. No one in Washington had heeded Eisenhower's warning. It would prove to be a costly mistake as we went into another country's revolution that was no threat to our national security.

In the hundred years since the end of the Civil War the makeup of the Democratic and Republican Parties literally reversed. African Americans who had initially flocked to the Republican Party because Lincoln had saved them, now switched to the Democratic Party which was backing the Civil Rights Movement led by Dr. Martin Luther King, Jr. Hispanics, other minorities, and white women joined into both the Civil Rights Movement and anti-war movement with the Democrats. The Republican Party became the conservative "Hawks" who not only favored the Vietnam War but limited the effect of the Civil Rights Movement. Now all white Southerners, people in the Mid-West farming States, business oriented conservatives in the cities, and the Religious Right jumped on the Republican band wagon. With the election of 1968, the Republicans had a strong candidate in Richard Nixon and not only swept the White House but Congress as well. The Vietnam War went into overdrive as the protests at home grew more violent. The country was coming apart at the seams. More radical and violent revolutionary groups were springing up around the country. Everywhere young people were questioning the government and losing faith in it. President Nixon sensing that he would lose the 1972 election unless he made a bold move regarding the Vietnam War, in late 1971 devised a plan to "Bring the Boys

Home" and turn over the war to the South Vietnamese Army (ARVN). He ordered an immediate troop withdraw and by 1973 almost all-American troops were sent home. Unfortunately, for President Nixon, in his zeal to get re-elected he authorized his henchmen to break into the Democratic National Headquarters at the Watergate to gain valuable secrets to use against them in the upcoming election. He won the 1972 election by a landslide but soon his misdeeds were discovered, and he was forced out of Office. The inconsequential dirt he had stolen from the Democrats had cost him the Presidency by 1974. He would have won the election without it. Instead, he had to resign in disgrace. After Gerald Ford and Jimmy Carter came Ronald Reagan, the best Republican President since Abraham Lincoln. He was a true leader and a great inspiration to the American people. He ended the Cold War and brought about the collapse of the Communist Soviet Union (Russia). When Reagan was president, no country in the world challenged the United States for they knew Reagan would crush them. After Reagan, the Republicans could only muster lackluster Presidents such as George H.W. Bush, George W. Bush, and Donald Trump. The

Democrats were in the same boat electing Bill Clinton and Barack Obama. Reagan was a tough act to follow.

With the election of 2016, wherein Hillary Clinton and Donald Trump were the Democratic and Republic nominees, both parties' lost prestige. The question on everyone's mind was "Who is the lesser of the two evils?" The U.S. election for president had sunk to an all-time low with candidates using the "F word," calling each other horrible names, pulling dirty tricks on each other, spreading false lies about each other, and generally acting like a couple of pissed off children. What a classy campaign. The whole world was laughing at us and I was embarrassed to call myself an American.

Meanwhile, the great congressional standoff was going on between the parties starting in 2009 when Barack Obama became President. The "conflict and stagnation" that George Washington had warned us about had arrived. You see, the rich, conservative – pro white Republicans could not believe that a Black Man had become President of the United States. In Congress, they blocked every piece of legislation that President Obama and the Democrats tried to push through. So, from 2009 until Obama's term expired in 2017, nothing of significance happened in the U.S. Government as we were deadlocked. The only productive legislation was preventing General Motors and Chrysler Corporation from going bankrupt and modifying the mortgage banking laws to keep millions of bogus loans from being foreclosed upon. Big losers – the American middle-class taxpayers.

Not to be outdone, the liberal, world citizen, rainbow warrior Democrats could not believe after the 2016 election that a White Nationalist Billionaire Outsider had become President of the United States. So, from 2017 until the present, nothing of significance has happened in the U.S. Congress as the Democrats have blocked every piece of legislation that President Trump and the Republicans have proposed. Once again, the American people are the big losers. But the Democrats could not stop their vengeance by simply blocking Republican backed legislation. No, they made it their personal mission to get that "Liar Trump" out of office. They spent millions of your taxpayer dollars on their personal vendetta of investigation after investigation of the President culminating in the Impeachment Farce. The trial in the Senate was absolutely incompetent. The Democratic prosecution did not call any live witnesses nor did they produce any authenticated documentary evidence. They should have subpoenaed the witnesses, documents, e-mails, and phone calls prior to commencing the trial. By only introducing prior Congressional hearing statements and documents not subject to cross examination they were in effect, entering inadmissible hearsay as their evidence. As the prosecutors, the burden was on them as to how they should make their case. They should have simply started calling subpoenaed witnesses to the witness stand to testify instead of putting it to vote by a Republican controlled Senate. It is like trying a defendant for robbery with no live witness testimony. The Judge would immediately grant a Judgement of Acquittal as the case was not proven. This is exactly what happened in the Senate Impeachment Trial – not proven.

There was also the obvious math problem involved with the trial. In order to convict the President, the Democratic prosecutors would need 67 out of 100 votes. Since it was obvious from the start that everyone was going to vote on party lines with the exception of a few possible cross over votes, the maximum votes the Democrats could have hoped for was 51. Now, any competent prosecutor would know that if you must have 67 votes to convict, but at best you are only going to get 51, then why bother to tie up the entire legislative and governmental process of the country for nearly two weeks on a guaranteed loser? The answer is obvious – it was 2020 and an election year. So, the entire trial was a Giant Soap Opera for the American People to watch and come to the conclusion that Trump is a lying, cheating, sleaze and we need to vote for those good, honest, fabulous Democrats who are trying to protect us from those horrible Republicans in Washington. So what the Democrats got out of it was millions of dollars of free TV and multi-media time saying Vote for Us, Vote for Us, Vote for Us, because we are the Good Guys. Really?

To make matters worse it appears that in the 2020 Presidential Election, you voters are once again going to ask yourself, "Who is the lesser of the two evils?" We know Donald Trump and Mike Pence will be the Republican Candidates and Joe Biden and Kamala Harris have the Democratic Nominations. Once again, bad choices. Where are good, honest, common sense, middle class candidates when we need them? Without severe reform of the campaign laws for the President and Congress, the candidates will just continue to BUY the election by spending so much on media campaign ads that the public gets brain washed. Hitler and his Propaganda Minister, Joseph Gerbels used the same tactics to brain wash the German People into believing the Nazi Party was the answer to their hopes and dreams. By 1945, Germany was destroyed, and millions of Germans lay dead. Lying politicians will tell you anything you want to hear to get you to follow them. Let's found a political party who not only tells you the truth but has provable facts to back up what they say instead of hollow promises like the Democrats and Republicans.

The problems facing our government are never ending. Right after the Impeachment Farce here comes COVID-19, or its common term "Coronavirus." This was the "Christmas Surprise" promised by North Korean leader Kim Jong Un just before Christmas, 2019. Everyone was waiting for a long-range ballistic missile test to fall in the Pacific Ocean just off the California Coast or an underground nuclear test. But nothing happened. We all breathed a sigh of relief figuring Kim was just running his mouth. But was he? I believe the "Christmas Surprise" was the COVID-19 virus. Before you dismiss me as insane, please hear me out.

The Coronavirus originated in China just around Christmas time. The first three countries to report cases of it shortly after Christmas were China, South Korea, and Iran. Who are the three countries who were angry with the United States in late 2019 due to tariffs or economic sanctions being placed upon them? Do China, North Korea, and Iran come to mind? China was in a tariff war with President Trump. North Korea's economy was in chaos due to all the sanctions imposed upon them by the United States and they felt President Trump had promised to lift those sanctions and then double crossed them by failing to do so. Iran had huge economic sanctions, oil embargos, the killing of their top General by the U.S., and had nearly gone to war with us. So let's suppose for the sake of discussion that the best Chemical/Biological warfare specialists from these three countries had met in secret in a sophisticated laboratory in China and developed a mutation of the Coronavirus into COVID-19 in order to destroy the United States economy as pay back. However, several of these scientists had accidentally contracted the virus and unintentionally spread it to their own people. Hence the first three countries to report cases are China, South Korea, and Iran. But wait... that's "South which will allow the Chinese, North Koreans, and Iranians to take us over economically and ultimately militarily. The Dollar will collapse, and no longer be the world money standard. Millions of Americans will die from the fear, paranoia, and violence brought on by the COVID-19 virus and its aftermath. This is their battle plan and if you Americans do not stop panicking over this virus, you will fall into their trap. It is time to remember the old saying, "When the going gets tough, the tough get going." Or as Benjamin Franklin put it in 1776: "They who can give up essential liberty to obtain a little temporary safety, deserve neither liberty nor safety." Sometimes you must tighten your belt, give up some luxuries, change your lifestyle, and get in shape in order to get through hard economic times. The American people had real rough times during the Great Depression of the 1930's and World War II. They showed incredible courage and self-sacrifice under far worse conditions than some man-made virus could produce. Yet, you all are panicking and fearful of what will happen. Put on a pair of gloves, a face mask, and stay 6 feet apart. Oh, but then I will look foolish and everyone will not be able to see how cute I am. Get over yourself and think about society as a whole. When the

A COMMONSENSE APPROACH TO GOVERNMENT THAT A "REAL PARTY" SHOULD PURSUE

IN 1776, THE GREAT PATRIOT, Thomas Paine wrote "Common Sense" in order to arouse the American Colonists against the King of England, George III, and the oppressive laws passed against them by Parliament at the King's request. While analyzing the colonist's relationships with Great Britain, he made an eloquent series of observations as follows:

"Alas, we have been long led away by ancient prejudices, and made large sacrifices to superstition. We have boasted the protection of Great Britain, without considering, that her motive was interest not attachment; that she did not protect us from our enemies on our account, but from her enemies on her own account, from those who had no quarrel with us on any other account, and who will always be our enemies on the same account. Let Britain waive her pretensions to the continent, or the continent throw off the dependence, and we should be at peace with France and Spain were they at war with Britain."

In simple terms – what he was saying was the British picked and chose the colonists enemies for them, and made them go to war against those enemies, not for the colonist's best interests, but for Britain's best interest. The big winners in wealth and power were the British. The biggest losers in manpower and destruction of property were the colonists. Sound familiar? Other than World War II, which was thrust upon us by Japanese and German aggression, what other modern wars or limited actions thrust upon us by Washington were really in the American people's best interest? Korea? Lebanon? Dominican Republic? Vietnam? Panama? Bosnia? Herzegovina? Gulf 1 – Kuwait and Iraq? Somalia? Haiti? Serbia? Afghanistan? Gulf 2 – Iraq, Syria, and ISIS? Nigeria?

Of all of the above in my opinion, only Gulf 1 – the invasion of Kuwait by Iraq, and the invasion of Afghanistan in retaliation for the attacks on the World Trade Center and the Pentagon, were in the best interests of the people of the United States. All the others were interventions by the U.S. Military into civil wars between rival factions in independent countries where we had no business going. We need to let the populace in foreign countries work out their internal problems and not intervene. We cannot afford financially and the further loss of American lives to right the wrongs of the world. In short, we need to stop playing World Policemen. If these people don't have the internal fortitude to protect themselves and fight their own battles, why the hell should we do it for them? I, for one, am sick of it. The Military-Industrial Complex, on the other hand loves it.

Thomas Paine would further write in "The Crisis" in December of 1776, when The Revolutionary War was in its infancy, prophetic words to try to bolster the American fighting spirit as the war was not going well at the time: "These are the times that try men's souls: The summer soldier and the sunshine patriot will, in the crisis, shrink from the service of his country; but he that stands it now, deserves the love and thanks of man and woman. Tyranny, like hell, is not easily conquered; yet we have this consolation with us, that the harder the conflict, the more glorious the triumph. What we obtain too cheap, we esteem too lightly: 'Tis dearness only that gives everything its value. Heaven knows how to put a proper price upon its goods; and it would be strange indeed, if so celestial an article as run for President, Senator, and the House of Representatives. It does not make any difference if it is a Democratic or Republican candidate running for office, because they are all in the pockets of the power elite. Regardless of which one wins the election they must be responsible to the members of the power elite who got them elected. With the staggering expenses of running a modern-day election campaign, where does the money come from? Certainly not from the average citizens contribution of $5 to $20. Look at all the lobbyists in Congress peddling influence to your law makers so they will pass laws beneficial to huge financial institutions, banks, manufacturing facilities, drug companies, insurance companies, hospital chains, real estate holding companies, stock brokerage firms, auto makers, oil companies, and other multi-million dollar corporations. Are these lobbyists nothing more than "Fixers" who are guilty of nothing more than "Bribery?" Think about it – when I was a criminal defense lawyer, if I had gone to a Judge on behalf of my client and offered him a large sum of money to dismiss the charges against my client, it would have been a felony crime. Worse yet – upon being discovered both the Judge and I would be prosecuted, sent to jail, and disbarred from practicing law.

monies awarded to the final two or three candidates who have shown voter strength through the primaries and who end up in the final election. Where does the money come from? An election candidate's trust fund. If every taxpayer were assessed a voluntary $20.00 election campaign fee on his tax return, a huge amount of money could be raised. Furthermore, individual candidates could accept donations from individuals up to $100. However, no corporation, partnership, or other business entity could make a contribution to the candidate in its name. Not too many candidates would sell their integrity for $100. It would take a whole lot more than that.

What about the big states versus the little states? Obviously, a candidate from California who had two million voters in his district would receive 20 times as much money from the campaign trust fund as a candidate from Maine who only had one hundred thousand voters in his district. The rules for distributing the money would have to be worked out by people with commonsense, integrity, and honesty. The candidates would be limited on the amount of TV and Radio air time they could purchase, so the rest of us could give our eyes and ears a break around election time, instead of the endless blitz of distasteful, negative ads that are attempting to brain wash us. The Democrats and Republicans will not vote for such an election system as it will cause them to go back to traditional campaign methods like walking the neighborhoods and shaking hands with common people. Oh, how horrible.

The power elite who control the Democrats and Republicans even put a reminder for you on the back of the One Dollar Bill. On the flip side from George Washington's portrait is a pyramid with the "all seeing eye" on top. This eye, of course, represents them sitting high above the rest of us who are the blocks of the pyramid holding them up. If you don't believe it, feel free to review the economic statistics of the United States that show that approximately 80 percent of the wealth generated by the U.S. economy goes to the top two percent of the population. That means that the other 98 percent of the population is scrounging for the left-over 20 percent of the money. The words on top of the pyramid Annuit Coeptis mean "favors our undertakings" and the words on the bottom Novus Ordo Seclorum mean "new order of the ages." The Roman Poet Virgil wrote those phrases during the heyday of the Roman Empire. Of course, the Roman Empire was only "favored" and a "new order" until 410 A.D., when the Visigoth King Alaric conquered and sacked Rome ending in its total destruction by 476 A.D.

A brief history of the Roman Empire will reveal one that is in many ways similar to that of the United States. Rome had humble beginnings as a small city state in Central Italy. By 300 B.C. it had either conquered or allied itself with all other city states on the Italian Peninsula and rose to prominence. By 264 B.C. the Carthaginians, who had a powerful city state in northern Africa that dominated the trade routes of the Mediterranean Sea, were at war with Rome. Twenty three years later, the war ended with Rome the eventual victor. However, by 218 B.C. a second war started when the Carthaginians under Hannibal attacked Italy from the North and won numerous victories almost taking Rome itself. The Romans then attacked Carthaginian colonies in Spain and went on to threaten Carthage. This forced Hannibal to leave Italy to defend his city resulting in an overwhelming victory by the Romans in 202 B.C. The victory allowed the Romans to dictate humiliating peace terms and seize control of the lucrative Mediterranean trade routes. While Carthage continued to survive, she was but a shell of her past glory and when she violated some of the terms of the peace agreement Rome voided it. In 146 B.C., they attacked Carthage, slaughtered most of the inhabitants and burned her to the ground. Rome was now master of the Mediterranean Sea. Rome spread eastward, either conquering or occupying by treaty all of Greece, Macedonia, Turkey, and parts of the Persian Empire in the Middle East. By 133 B.C. Rome had evolved into a Republic with a Senate ruling body made up of the wealthy and powerful patricians (like our Senate) and the Plebeians, who were common people without titles, but still had power and wealth due to their positions of influence in Roman Society (like our House of Representatives). Two Consuls formed the Executive Branch, one usually a little more powerful than the other due to persuasive abilities (like our President and Vice President). In effect, our government was founded on many of the same principles as the Roman Republic.

In 105 B.C. the Romans lost two armies in a military disaster at the hands of several hundred thousand Gaulish tribesmen in Southern France. Had the Gauls headed south for Rome they probably would have taken it and changed the course of history. However, they made the mistake of heading west for Spain giving the Romans time to raise new armies and re-equip them. By 101 B.C. they caught up with the Gauls and annihilated them.

In 59 B.C. a rising young star named Julius Caesar had politically maneuvered himself into a position of power as a Consul, along with two older generals, Pompey and Crassus. In a stroke of genius, he volunteered as governor of the province of Gaul and left Rome to confront a new rebellion by Gaulish Tribesmen. Over a period of seven years, Caesar using brilliant military tactics and recruiting defeated Gauls into his army, conquered all of Gaul (modern day France), made incursions into Germany, and sent raiding parties into Britain. Caesar had become a national hero while Crassus had died and Pompey sat idly in Rome. In 49 B.C. Pompey and the Senate had declared Caesar an enemy of the State fearing his popularity amongst the people. When the news reached him in Gaul, Caesar and his legions crossed the River Rubicon, which was forbidden by Roman law, and headed for Rome. Pompey, knowing his army was no match for Caesar's, fled eastwards. Caesar followed and destroyed Pompey's army in Greece in 48 B.C. He then moved through the Middle East into Egypt and took more territory in North Africa and Spain. When he returned triumphantly to

Rome, he was appointed dictator by the Senate for the next 10 years. However, the appointment would be cut short, when in 44 B.C. numerous Senators stabbed him to death as he entered the Senate because they knew he had too much power. His successor, Augustus Caesar, then defeated several political rivals in battles as far away as Egypt and became the first Emperor of the Republic. The Senate was now reduced to "Yes Men" approving Augustus' every dictate. For the next 150 years Rome would be at peace, albeit under the iron fisted rule of its Emperors. Its empire would circle the Mediterranean Sea on land and stretch to the north into France, Germany, and Britain. It would control all Western Civilization at the time and have a lasting effect on the language, science, religion, architecture, art, government, literature, wars, and roads of Western Europe. But for all the good it produced, it also was responsible for the evils associated with greed, wealth, and power that we see in Western Civilization today.

The next 150 years of peace, called Pax Romana, also brought with it a total decline in the military strength, morals, sexual practices, religious beliefs, work habits, education, family ties, and ethics, of the Roman citizens. They went from hard working, energetic, fearless, militaristic, ethical, and self-ruling people to lazy, lackluster, unwilling to fight for their country, greedy, unethical people, self-absorbed in pleasure, and indifferent to rule by their Emperor. You see, they were too busy in the pleasures of Roman life to realize they had given up their right to rule themselves via a Republic and had handed all power over to an Emperor who promised them "Bread and Circus." A great Colosseum was built in central Rome which could seat 50,000 spectators beginning in 70 A.D. by Emperor Vespasian. The construction took several years to complete. One of his sons, Emperor Domitian, was a ruler who understood the importance of pacifying the people with games and spectacles in the Colosseum. He also distracted them with great building projects such as markets, temples, and housing, as well as making personal donations from the treasury to every citizen. Great gladiatorial combats were presented on a regular basis where teams of men would fight to the death to the cheers of the blood thirsty spectators. Do the Ultimate Fighting Championships, National Football League, and World Boxing Association come to mind? Great chariot races where expensive chariots drown by the fastest horses in the realm would race stretched from England, France, and Spain in the West to the Mesopotamia (modern day Iraq) in the East. Since the territory it governed had grown so large, it became extremely difficult for the Roman Legions to defend its borders. Constant incursions by outside Barbarian Tribes and internal revolts within some of the conquered nations such as the Hebrews (modern day Israel) required the Roman rulers to change their thinking. They now implemented a plan whereby non-Roman citizens such as Guals, Goths, Visigoths, Slavs, and Vandals could serve in the Roman Army with promises of payments in gold and silver and eventual Roman citizenship. In effect, instead of the citizen army motivated by the love of the State and Family, they now had a mercenary army motivated by self-gain with no loyalty to Rome whatsoever. Worse yet, by equipping the paid soldiers with the latest weapons and armor, and teaching them the battle formations and tactics that had made the Roman Legions so formidable, they were in effect teaching their enemies how to beat Rome at its own game. Prime example – King Alaric, who had been in the Roman Army and rose to prominence with numerous victories leading Visigoth Legions in the Eastern part of the Empire against Barbarian incursions became dissatisfied with the Roman government. After the Emperor refused to promote him to General and repudiated numerous promises made to his men, Alaric went on the attack taking numerous cities in Northern Italy and finally capturing and sacking Rome itself. The superb military training he had received from the Romans now came back to haunt them. Rome was further sacked by the Vandals in 455 A.D. and finally succumbed to Germanic Barbarian rule in 476 A.D., when King Odoacer deposed the last Roman Emperor. The mightiest government on earth with the greatest army and navy on earth was no more. The population of the City of Rome went from over one million people to less than thirty thousand people in the next 100 years as all of Europe was plunged into the Dark Ages.

Historians have outlined eight major reason why Rome fell:

1. A string of military losses sustained against outside Barbarian forces after 300 A.D. because the Roman Army no longer had a majority of citizen soldiers but recruited more mercenaries from amongst non-Roman peoples. In effect, they were substituting soldiers of inferior quality because Roman citizens no longer

wanted to fight for their country. They were too caught up in the pleasures of life. Sound Familiar?

2. Economic problems and reliance on slave labor. When the Empire stopped expanding its borders after 200 A.D., its chief source of income as a result of plundering conquered countries and sending thousands of their citizens back to Rome as slaves dried up. Constant wars and overspending by the Emperors had almost bankrupted the imperial treasury. Since the economy depended on slaves to perform all the physically demanding tasks of farming, construction, repairing, crafting, and loading vessels of commerce, when the fresh influx of slaves dried up, the Empire was hit by a shortage of laborers. This added to the financial deficit causing the government to raise taxes and lessen the gold and silver content in its coins resulting in severe inflation. The gap between the wealthy, who still had the means to avoid taxes and acquire slaves, and the common citizen continued to widen. As time progressed more "middle class" Romans found themselves in the ranks of the poor. The once thriving sea trade routes

were gradually being taken over by rival countries and threatened by roving bands of pirates. So, lack of Romans' willing to work, financial crisis brought about by wars, taxation, inflation, and loss of favorable trade routes were a major factor in Rome's decline. Sound familiar?

3. The portioning of the Empire into two halves, one in the West and one in the East. Shortly after 300 A.D. Emperor Constantine moved his seat of power from Rome to Byzantium in modern day Turkey. The city would later be renamed Constantinople in his honor and rise to great prominence and wealth. At first having a Co-Emperor in Rome made governing the Empire easier, but over time the two factions started squabbling against each other instead of cooperating. The Western part of the Empire spoke Latin and were largely Catholic Christians whereas the Eastern Empire spoke Greek and followed the Orthodox form of Christianity. As the Eastern Empire grew in wealth and power, the Western portion declined. This was noticed by Barbarian tribes outside both Empires who attacked the weaker Western

half with impunity and stayed away from Constantinople due to its impregnable fortifications. By splitting its forces Rome failed to heed Julius Caesar's famous strategy of "divide and conquer" your enemy. Likewise, the United States has split its armed forces by putting large military forces in Europe, the Balkans, and the Middle East, while also putting large amounts of forces in Japan, South Korea, and Guam half a world away. Also, the Democrat vs. Republican fight has definitely split the U.S. in two as apparently one is speaking Latin while the other is speaking Greek.

4. Extending its Empire too far and military overspending were primary factors in Rome's collapse. Because the Empire was so physically large it presented an administrative and logistical nightmare for the people charged with governing it. Roman Legions were spread thinly from Britain to Mesopotamia, requiring Emperor Hadrian to build his famous wall between England and Scotland. As more money was spent on the military, technological advancement was checked and Rome's

internal infrastructure such as bridges, roads, buildings, and aqueducts fell into disrepair. Sound familiar?

5. Government corruption and political instability were major contributors to Rome's downfall. Countless Roman Emperors were killed by rivals wanting the position for themselves during the first 200 years after Julius Caesar's death. Civil Wars and Rebellions led to constant changes of Emperors during this time frame making the Emperor's job the most dangerous. The Roman Senate added to the lack of clear direction for the government due to corruption and incompetence within their ranks. The average Roman citizen lost all sense of trust in the Emperor and Senate causing them to question the policies of the leadership. Sound familiar? The countless attacks by an incompetent Congress on President Trump have the same result. And could there be any "corruption" in Washington, D.C.?

6. Allowing Barbarian tribes from without the Empire to immigrate into the Empire due to Attila the Hun's invasion of Eastern Europe. The Visigoths and Goths were being pushed westward and southward out of

Romania and Germany by Atilla the Hun and his advancing Hun hordes to the borders of the Roman Empire. They implored the Romans to let them in lest they be slaughtered by Atilla's men. The Romans reluctantly let them into the Empire but put harsh restrictions on them and required them to serve in the Roman Army. Ultimately the Visigoths under King Alaric attacked and looted Rome in 410 A.D. They were one of the tribes the Romans let in to escape Atilla's wrath. If this doesn't sound familiar, you've obviously missed all the news regarding: thousands of refugees from Central America and Mexico demanding political asylum in the United States due to gang violence in their countries; the wall proposed by President Trump; and the thousands of Syrian, Iraqi, and Afghan refugees wanting asylum in the United States to escape ISIS, the Talaban, and other Arab Terrorists. Same situation that the Roman's faced. Same lack of loyalty to their new government.

7. Christianity and the loss of traditional values. Emperor Constantine became a Christian and in 313 A.D. decreed

that the Christians should no longer be persecuted for practicing their religion. By 380 A.D. it had become the official religion of the Empire. Some historians felt that once Christianity replaced the ancient Roman Gods that the loyalty of the citizens shifted away from the Emperor, who was supposedly a God on Earth, to the Church which taught that Jesus was the Son of God, there was only one true God and the Romans former Pagan beliefs were heresy. This took the wind out of the ancient tales of Roman God-like heroes who had been aided in battle by the Gods to overcome an insurmountable enemy. Suddenly these old tales of glory became childish fairy tales not worthy of consideration by the citizenry of Rome. Apparently, these historians are saying that the teachings of Jesus regarding brotherly love, humility, and the prohibition against killing a fellow man, took the fight out of the Romans adding to their downfall. The opposite is true in the U.S. today because we have forsaken the teachings of Jesus Christ and the Bible and worship material things as Gods causing us to lose our moral compass and indulge ourselves in pleasurable pursuits.

8. Because of numerous reasons listed above, the Roman Legions began to change from being well trained and disciplined Roman citizens within their ranks to foreign paid mercenaries with no loyalty to Rome who were not as motivated as the original Legions when in battle. The Visigoths, Goths, and Vandals who sacked Rome in 410, 455, and 476 A.D. were all former Roman Legionnaires. Today, the United States Armed Forces are facing similar issues. We need to reinstate the Draft for United States citizens to serve again.

It would seem that the aforesaid eight issues that brought down Rome, are the same as those facing the United States today.

How to avoid the same pitfalls of Rome by the formation of a strong dedicated party responsible to the Middle Class who carry the loads and burdens of the country.

We need to bring back compulsory military service for all males aged 18 to 25. Females who want to go into the military can simply join the volunteer military services and sign up for the normal four-year commitment. All other females who do not want to join the military will not be drafted. The draft should be a short one – six months to one year. Afterward, the draftee shall have to serve in the reserves and attend one day of training per month for 2 years to keep their skills sharp. It is time we put manly pursuits back into our boys and create a competent second layer of citizen soldiers to back up our professional military. Switzerland had a similar system of compulsory military training for all males and it kept Hitler from invading them in 1940. His Generals told him that the Swiss men could mobilize within hours and were very well trained and German losses would be so heavy that they might not be victorious. Hitler reluctantly called off the invasion. Instead of sending all of our military money overseas to train other countries soldiers, we need to train our own boys to become Minutemen in defense of the United States. It also causes an 18-year-old undisciplined boy to become a responsible, self-confident man. Society as a whole benefits as traditionally men who have served in the military do better in civilian life. But hey – let's continue to spend all of our time and money training the Afghans and Iraqi's how to wage war.

The healthcare dilemma can be sensibly compromised. We need to study other countries healthcare systems. A combination of private hospitals and insurance for those who can pay the freight can be combined with government hospitals and medical staff for those who cannot. It would seem that Austria, England, Canada, and Denmark have split systems, private and government, that seem to work. The United States could start a civilian health care system similar to that of the military. The government pays a student's tuition to attend medical school and they owe the government six years of service as a doctor in a government hospital in return. Do not worry about the quality of the medical service – it will be the same as the military hospitals who do an excellent job. Of course, there will have to be a fiscally responsible way to pay for it and that will take research to reach the best result. I can assure you the best result is not the building of hospitals in the Middle East in order that government contractors make high profits as pay back for supporting certain elected officials. The trillions of dollars going to the war efforts in Iraq and Afghanistan could pay for a whole lot of health care here in the United States. Hey Washington, D.C., get out of the Middle East.

We need to revamp our public educational system. We are spending so much money on building, maintaining, or repairing dilapidated school buildings it is absurd. Transportation of students on buses is another huge expense that could be significantly reduced. The COVID-19 situation has produced a system wherein children can take classes online at home. While this is not the total solution, a compromise system could be worked out where some students could learn at home while others attended smaller, cheaper schools much closer to their homes which would cut transportation costs significantly. Recommendations of experienced educators not politicians on how to implement a dual school education system – part time on line and part time in classrooms should be developed and followed.

We need to change our election laws to allow members of the House of Representatives to serve 4 year terms instead of having to run for re-election every two years. The costs of a re-election campaign every two years are staggering. In order to raise the money needed for a campaign every two years, Congressmen (or Congresswomen) must make promises to pass certain laws that benefit corporate contributors. Why not change their terms to 4 years, but with a 12 year cap on their total time in Congress? Senators only have to run for re-election every 6 years. So they also should be limited to a 12 year cap in the Senate. The President stays at two 4 year terms for a total of 8 years. By putting term limits on everyone in Washington, D.C., you accomplish several important goals. With a new influx of Senators and Congressmen every 12 years no one gets addicted to the Washington syndrome. You actually have new representatives of the people from the States with new ideas and energy to move the country forward, instead of dinosaurs and fossils who have forgotten which state they are representing. Oh that's right… it's the District of Columbia a/k/a the City of Washington. We need fresh blood infused into our Federal government.

Our tax system needs complete readjustment. The IRS and Federal Income Tax needs to go. The IRS is a self-serving money loser. We do not need Federal Income Taxes – we need to come up with a sensible way to administer a national sales tax of 10% on all goods and services provided in this country. For example, a drug dealer buys a nice new $45,000.00 car and since he does not pay income tax on his ill-gotten gains the Federal Government gets $0.00 from him. With a national sales tax the government immediately gets $4,500.00 from the sale of that car. Since he will be using the local interstate (Federal Highway) to transport his drugs, why should he not help pay for the maintenance and upkeep of the road like the rest of us? Likewise, an illegal immigrant working for cash "under the table" will pay no income taxes. But if he goes out and buys a $30,000.00 truck to haul his produce, he's got to pay $3,000.00 to the Feds. My solution is simple. If you do not want to buy any products, goods, or services, then you don't have to pay any federal taxes. Of course, you'll have to live out in the woods in a hut without electricity, water, sewer, a car, satellite TV, or any other modern convenience. Since most Americans like to live in luxury and comfort, I do not think the Federal tax revenues will suffer. Even the rich will have to pay their fair share (for a change) because when they buy that multimillion-dollar house, Rolls Royce, Ferrari, or airplane, you guessed it, 10% goes to the Federal Government. Now everyone is paying their fair share. How do you enforce this new sales tax? First, dissolve the IRS and hire some intelligent and energetic people who monitor the sales data of stores, businesses, and corporations and insure they are remitting the 10% tax to the Feds instead of pocketing it for themselves. Make the penalties so incredibly harsh that no business wants to risk it. It will not be a simple pay back to the Feds of the money owed to them plus penalties and interest like the current situation if you're behind on your taxes. No, it will be like the drug forfeiture laws where the business owner goes to prison for a minimum mandatory term of years and the business is seized by the government and sold to new owners at auction. Knowing they will go to prison and forfeit the business is a clear incentive for them to collect the National Sales Tax and remit it to the government. But what about the Social Security deduction from your paycheck? It will only be made if you elect to participate in the Social Security Program. You can opt out and elect to use a private retirement plan. But you say won't that cause the Social Security System to bankrupt eventually? Yes it will, but it's going to run out of money anyway. Why not let the government subsidize it with the trillions of dollars it will be saving by getting our military out of all the aforesaid third world countries where they should not be to begin with.

Now let's move on to the big one – the U.S. National Debt. If you have ever been to Jekyll Island, Georgia, you have been to the birthplace of income tax, and the Federal Reserve System.

Some of the richest families in America became members of the Jekyll Island Club started by Newton Finney, John Claflin, and members of the Du Bignon family into which Finney had married. Soon they were selling investment shares in the Club to members of the Union Club in New York City which included the wealthiest men in the country as members. The fledging Jekyll Island Club now had members such as J.P. Morgan, Pierre Lorilland, William Vanderbilt, Joseph Pulitzer, Lloyd Aspinwall, Marshall Field, George Pullman, Judge Henry Howland, William Rockefeller, Wirt Dexter, and Andrew Carnegie who were the "who's who" of their day in 1886. Later a continual list of newer wealthy members would join the Club – including Edwin Gould and the Astor Family. By 1901, when Theodore Roosevelt became President of the United States, the Club's members had more combined net worth than the U.S. Government. These people controlled the banks, steel mills, railroads, oil production, manufacturing plants, food distribution networks, newspapers, department stores, cotton mills, shipping industry, stock markets, real estate trusts, mining, coal production, electrical utilities, water works, phone utilities, radio and telegraph communications, insurance companies, and any other money making schemes you can think of. In effect they owned the U.S. Economy. Being members of the same club they would meet after dinner in the cigar smoked library sipping the best alcoholic beverages of the day and discuss business and politics. Remember, these were the smartest and most ruthless businessmen of their day. So when they decided to take out and bankrupt a smaller business competitor it was like the New York Yankees taking on a Little League baseball team – no contest.

President Theodore Roosevelt and his government lawyers took note of these high powered business men taking out these smaller businesses on a regular basis and soon stepped in to stop these "Robber Barons" as he called them from putting all small businesses out of business. A series of anti-trust laws were passed in Congress giving the Government the power to break up these business monopolies and financial trusts. If you have ever played the board game "Monopoly" by Parker Brothers, the character of the little old man with the grey mustache and the black top hat is a likeness of J.P. Morgan, who in the early 1900's was the richest man in the world. Soon numerous club members such as J.P. Morgan,

George Baker, James Hill, and William Rockefeller were subpoenaed to appear before the House Committee on Banking and Currency. Meanwhile, government lawyers were filing lawsuits to break up the business monopolies and financial trusts owned by the club members. The members had enough of these upstart government politicians and lawyers interfering with their private business interests and decided to strike back in an extremely intelligent and underhanded way. They enlisted the aid of Senator Nelson Aldrich of Rhode Island who agreed to meet with them at the Jekyll Island Club to discuss a central banking system with the ready reserves to financially back the U.S. Governments' need for loans in times of financial crisis. This was the beginning of the Federal Reserve Banking System on which the government relies today. In December 1913, Congress enacted and approved the Federal Reserve System. The inner circle of billionaires had won the day and mortgaged the U.S. Government. What started as a slow process of lending was soon accelerated by World War I, the Great Depression, World War II, the Korean War, the Arms Race with Russia, the Vietnam War, financial recessions over the years, the Persian Gulf Wars, the War in Afghanistan, trade deficits with China, and COVID-19 (just to name a few causes of our debt) resulting in a huge national debt. Who are the big winners – the families who own the banks that control the interest rates charged by the Federal Reserve System. Who are the big losers – everyone else in the U.S. who pays taxes - You see – these guys are like loan sharks who have lent the government so much money, with interest, that it can never be repaid. So from now until the U.S. collapses under its own financial debt it will keep paying and paying the interest on the loans dating back over 100 years. As of July, 2020, the National Debt was 26 trillion dollars. Even the average citizen who gets into credit card debt paying 25 percent interest, which he or she will never be able to repay, has debt relief remedies such as bankruptcy or settling for 33 cents on the dollar owed. But not the U.S. government as it is under the control of the rich billionaires to which the national debt is partially owed, and the Federal Reserve System which is controlled by them, and possibly foreign bankers such as England's House of Rothchild banking dynasty, Germany's Norddeutsche Landesbank, and huge U.S. financial giants, Chase Manhattan Bank, and Goldman, Sachs of New York. Why do I say "possibly?" The Federal Reserve Laws as written make this to happen one way or another. These people have already fleeced this nation dry. Like King George and the British in Parliament in 1776, they need to go "Bye Bye." The U.S. Dollar used to be backed by gold until 1933, when it went on the silver standard. By 1963, we were on the "Federal Reserve Note" standard meaning that your U.S. Dollar is now backed by... I'm not sure but it sounds like a "promissory note" to a bunch of filthy rich bankers. And of course now we have all this "computer money" backed by electronic programs, which when subjected to an EMP Attack by China, North Korea, or Iran (or all three together) will result in Catastrophic Monetary failures causing you, the American Citizen, to lose all the money in your bank account.

So, our party pledge would be to immediately get the sharpest anti-cyber-attack people on this problem and set up an EMP proof grid system. Where, you say does this money come from and I say from the trillions of dollars we are saving by immediately withdrawing all U.S. Armed Forces from the Middle East, the Balkans, Africa, and several other small countries in Central and South America where we do not need to be. Pull out your history books or look it up on your computer and you will see that we are following the exact same pattern that the Roman Empire did resulting in its downfall. We can neither save nor govern the world. This idea of "world citizenship" is fostered by those who either want to make lots of money for themselves in foreign lands or by idealists who neither know nor understand world history. Hell, we can't even govern or save ourselves at this point unless we make serious changes, so how are we going to save the world? Our policy will be to only consider the defense of our United States and our closest Allies such as Britain, France, Canada, Belgium, the Netherlands, Denmark, Italy, Germany, Austria, Japan, and South Korea. Everyone else can fend for themselves and do their own fighting. We cannot support the world militarily and financially as it will bleed us dry. Our new party will only put the American Middle Class first. Hey, why not have a new U.S. Dollar that says "Federal Assets <u>Certificate</u>" instead of "Federal Reserve <u>Note</u>?"

What about Environmental and Global Warming concerns. These are real problems confronting our Nation even if some politicians want to dismiss them as "Hogwash". They will not be a quick fix like everyone wants, for example, banning all internal combustion vehicles and going to all electric vehicles. It will take time but eventually scientific research will find a solution to our environmental and catastrophic weather problems. Our party would pledge support and grants to the researchers who are trying to save the country from environmental calamities.

There are hundreds of other problems facing our nation too numerous to list but needing the attention of a party that puts the middle class first, not the rich and famous. For example, another thing our Party will cause to happen would be a full review of all Federal Laws. A group of well-educated and honest lawyers, businessmen, and historians could recommend the repeal or modification of laws that have become obsolete, or overlap each other, or contain "pork barrel" clauses designed to enrich special interest groups. That would probably result in the repeal of fifty percent of the Federal Laws. Good riddance! If you are a good, honest, hardworking American with common sense we want you to volunteer to join the Real Party of America. We do not want any racial bigots in our party, as we feel that you should not be judged by what DNA lies within your body, but what intelligence, honor, loyalty, and integrity lies within your body. Your outward appearance is only for strangers to see, but enough to participate in the 2020 Election. However, it should be up and running enough by 2024 to get some candidates elected. It will take time, but I believe if the American people have the intestinal fortitude to make the biggest change in American politics since 1854, that eventually the Real Party of American can make a dramatic change in the course this country is set upon. Hopefully, sooner than later they can change the balance of power in Congress and get one of our party members elected President. But we must abandon this Global domination idea that President Eisenhower warned us against. We are not the United States of the World. We are the United States of America.

Last, but not least, what about the Presidential election of 2020? Excellent question. Once again it would appear we have the same question of who is the lesser of the two evils that we had in 2016 when Hillary Clinton ran against Donald Trump. Joe Biden and Kamala Harris will be the Democratic Nominees and Donald Trump and Mike Pence will be the Republican Nominees. So here we go, my analysis:

Donald Trump is a Billionaire who got there through some shady real estate dealings and some honest ones. He is totally egotistical having even called himself "The chosen one" while pointing to the sky. His tweeting and texting are like those of a ninth grader. I have studied Adolph Hitler extensively and can tell you that Donald Trump exhibits many of the same personality traits and political showmanship as did Hitler. Like Hitler, he is not always truthful to the people. He needs to tone down a bit, stop using the "F word" in public, and get a little smoother in foreign relations instead of acting like a bully. The counter to the above things I do not like about him personally is that he does not take any static from the Washington political establishment, the Chinese, North Koreans, or Iranians. He also is very knowledgeable in financial affairs and business matters which has been excellent for the economy and made Wall Street confident. The current COVID-19 crisis has put a temporary damper on our economy but that is not Trump's fault as the Chinese, North Koreans, and Iranians sent that to us on purpose. The economy will make a rebound and my suggestion to Donald Trump would be if you do get re-elected make life hell for the Chinese, North Koreans, and Iranians. I also like the fact that he supports my firearms and 2nd Amendment Rights. Recent news reports have indicated that Russia favors President

Trump in the upcoming election while China and Iran prefer Joe Biden. (I'm sure North Korea also favors Biden although they have not said anything yet.)

Joe Biden seems like a very nice guy who may have made some political mistakes in the past when he voted certain ways on certain issues while in Congress. All of these mis-votes will come out during the campaign. Of course, there will also be accusations that his son's involvement in a questionable company in the Ukraine while he was Vice President of the United States violated some obscure law. Biden will counter that Trump should have been found guilty and impeached for asking the President of the Ukraine to investigate Biden and his son for their involvement in the aforesaid illicit company. There will be further accusations against him that he did not accomplish or do a lot as Vice-President. Joe Biden will counter that the whole COVID-19 thing is Donald Trump's fault because he did not react fast enough when it first came to the U.S., did not urge Governors to close down businesses, schools, court houses, and other public places soon enough, did not wear a mask in public, and generally said it was not that serious. He will also say that President Trump did not make the right decisions on how to fight the virus. The Republicans will then counter that when the Coronavirus first arrived it came in via cruise ships and airlines from China and Europe and President Trump put immediate travel bans on the countries from which it was coming. It seemed like the only "hot spots" were in Seattle, Los Angeles, and New York and the local officials seemed to be getting it under control. The President was trying to let the local officials handle it because he is a States Rights guy who thinks the federal government should only get involved when absolutely necessary. (You know like when demonstrators are destroying Portland, Oregon.) It would appear that Biden is more of an appeaser, like British Prime Minister Neville Chamberlin, whom Hitler chewed up and spit out at the Munich Peace Conference in 1936. Also, Biden favors gun control, which will only be the beginning of repealing the 2nd Amendment.

The question becomes why would Russia favor President Trump while China and Iran favor Joe Biden? I believe the answer is relatively obvious. While Russia and China used to be close allies in the 1950's and 1960's, as both countries pulled away from "pure" Communism to a modified capitalistic

Communism, their interests changed. Russia appears to have gone to a more democratic and capitalistic society then has China. Russia has realized that if they cooperate with the United States on certain military and economic agendas that the end result will be to Russia's benefit. Prime example – in Syria both Russia and the United States were bombing ISIS terrorists for different reasons. Russia was supporting the existing regime which the U.S. did not support. The U.S. was supporting the pro-democracy rebels which the Russians were against. However, both countries realized that ISIS was the worst threat to the entire Middle East and bombed them without mercy without stepping on each other's toes. End result, ISIS was eliminated to both country's benefit. I suggest we open lines of communication to the Russians on both military strategies to curb the Iranian terrorist threat in the Middle East and possible trade deals between us. Russia has huge oil reserves and mineral deposits which we could use. We have a huge capacity to manufacture products and grow agricultural products which the Russians could use. Why not start using American workers again instead of manufacturing everything in China and paying Chinese workers?

Speaking of which – China and Iran prefer Joe Biden because they know he is a appeaser who they can push around and get great treaties and trade agreements that they could never get from Donald Trump.

So, it's the Bully vs the Appeaser in the 2020 Presidential Election. Where's a candidate with the character, intelligence, and guts of Theodore Roosevelt when we need him?

Joe Biden has picked a Black woman, Kamala Harris, as his running mate. If he is elected, she will become the Vice President of the United States and then become President of the United States should he die or become incapacitated. In my opinion he has put himself in a very disadvantageous position because there are many militant feminist groups out there who want a woman leading the United States. Who is to say that these extreme feminists would not go to drastic measures to get Joe Biden out of the White House so they can get a woman in the White House? For example, if Mr. Biden had a mild stroke, which is very possible due to his age and pressures of the job, the feminists would immediately scream that he was incompetent to hold office so Kamala Harris and they could rule us. How would that change the Democratic agenda that Biden had put into place once he was gone? Things could change drastically. Just food for thought.

President Trump, on the other hand, has an experienced Vice President in Mike Pence, who has shown excellent leadership skills, has dealt with foreign leaders, and would follow Trump's agenda should anything happen to President Trump. Usually, the candidate's picks for a running mate are not so controversial and most people are not really concerned about who is second in command. But with Biden and Trump getting up there in age, and COVID-19 running rampant through the country, who is to say that either will make it through the next four years. So in this election the candidate's choices for Vice President are critical. It is obvious that Biden picked a black woman in order to get the black vote and the female vote, both of which are huge voting blocks. It could backfire on him with the rest of the population, who might be suspect of the ability of a black woman with no international diplomatic experience to lead the country, and change their vote to Trump. More food for thought.

The bottom line – regardless of which team wins, there still will not be enough changes made to rescue the middle class from its current dilemma. They still will be underpaid, overtaxed, and scrounging for whatever crumbs they can gather while the rich get richer. Our new proposed party will work to help the hard working middle class gain the economic power they deserve, so they can lead a better life. We intend to help the rich get a little poorer so the rest of us can get a piece of the economic pie.

We will penalize businesses who want to send all their manufacturing business to China, Southeast Asia, Mexico, Central America, India, Pakistan, and other Third World countries in order to take advantage of cheap labor rates so that those businesses can make exorbitant profits. We will make life extremely nice for those businesses who re-open manufacturing facilities in the United States and hire American workers. The greedy, unpatriotic, money lovers will find their businesses under fire daily from our Party. The Patriotic, pro-American businesses will find themselves getting government contracts and positive publicity. In other words, if you love China and all those other countries so much – we will gladly buy you a one-way plane ticket so you can live with "your people."

Recently, there was a huge explosion at a port in Lebanon

resulting in massive loss of life and property damage as a result of tons of fertilizer that was stored there. The fertilizer had been seized from a Russian ship several years prior to the explosion. While we all feel empathy for the plight of the Lebanese people, I was shocked to hear that the U.S. Government in sending 300 million dollars in relief aid to them. Why are we sending them all this money when we have roads, bridges, buildings, housing projects, historical sites, and countless other projects that need repairing here? Since this was Russian fertilizer, should not the Russians be offering the aid? Our Party policy will be to cut off aid to foreign countries, except in cases wherein U.S. security is at stake, and put that money back into the U.S. public works projects to bring us back to our former status.

By the time this book goes to press, there will be over 250,000 dead from the COVID-19 pandemic sent to us by the Chinese, North Koreans, and Iranians. So why are not millions of Americans marching in the streets demanding justice for our dead and urging everyone to stop buying Chinese products? Oh that's right – the Chinese products cost less at Walmart so its more important to save money than it is to retaliate against China for killing 250,000 of our people. Before you call me racist, I do not have a problem with the average Chinese citizen. I do have a huge problem with their dictatorial, murdering, militant government. The average Chinese citizen is just as much of a victim of that government as are the aforesaid dead Americans. Hey citizens of China – has is occurred to you that life would be much better if you had a government that was actually concerned with your welfare instead of their own? Maybe you should do something about that since I believe you greatly outnumber them.

As far as North Korea and Iran – we are not trading with them anyway so further economic sanctions are not necessary. The citizens who live in those countries need to fix the problem with their governments. We cannot do it for them. Our policy will be if they want to stop trying to destroy us and clean up their leadership mess, we will then deal with them in a civilized manner. It is their choice. The next move is in their court. What's it going to be? War or Peace?

CONCLUSION

THANK YOU FOR READING THIS book. I hope it gives you some insight as why things are the way they are in the United States of American at the present. If we would go back to our fundamental foundations upon which our country was founded such as "In God We Trust" and "All Men Are Created Equal" we would have a much better country then we have today. It's like the country in which I have grown up for the past 72 years has been HIJACKED by greedy businessmen and politicians. Hey, on September 11, 2001, were not four commercial airlines HIJACKED by Arab terrorists? And what happened to those four hijacked planes? They all got destroyed either purposely by the hijackers or unintentionally by citizen heroes who attempted to regain control of their hijacked plane. The result is always the same when an airplane gets hijacked – only a terrible destructive ending. What do you think the ending is for a country that has been hijacked? The 911 hijackers were Arab terrorists. The United States hijackers are greedy politicians and wealthy businessmen. Is there really a difference?

If you would like to volunteer to bring down those who have hijacked our American Democracy and put them out of the plane on a barren runway in the middle of a desert, join the Real Party of America. We need to mop up the Democrats and sweep out the Republicans before our system of government as envisioned by our Founding Fathers in 1789 perishes from the earth forever. Only you can make this happen.

POSTSCRIPT

Famous Common Sense Quotes

"We hold these truths to be self-evident, that all men are created equal." Thomas Jefferson, 1776

"Tyranny, like hell, is not easily conquered; yet we have this consolation with us, that the harder the conflict, the more glorious the triumph. What we obtain too cheap, we esteem too lightly." Thomas Paine, 1776

"Let us disappoint the men who are raising themselves upon the ruin of this country." Samuel Adams, 1776

"We must, indeed, all hang together, or most assuredly we shall all hang separately." Benjamin Franklin, 1776

"Political factions (modern day parties) may seek to obstruct the execution of the laws created by the government or to prevent the branches of government from exercising the powers provided them by the Constitution. Such factions may claim to be trying to answer popular demands to solve pressing problems, but their true intentions are to take the power from the people and place it in the hands of unjust men." George Washington's Farewell Address, 1796

"Observe good faith and justice towards all nations; cultivate peace and harmony with all. Religion and morality enjoin this conduct; and can it be, that good policy does not equally enjoin it? It will be worthy of a free, enlightened, and at no distant period, a great nation, to give to mankind the magnanimous and too novel example of a people always guided by an exalted justice and benevolence... Alas! Is it rendered impossible by its Vices?" George Washington's Farewell Address, 1796

"A house divided against itself cannot stand." Abraham Lincoln, 1861

"No man has a good enough memory to be a successful liar." Abraham Lincoln, date unknown

"You can please some of the people all of the time, you can please all of the people some of the time, but you can't please all the people all of the time." Abraham Lincoln, 1862

"To sit home, read one's favorite paper, and scoff at the misdeeds of the men who do things is easy, but it is markedly ineffective. It is what evil men count upon the good men's doing." Theodore Roosevelt, 1895

"I cannot consent to take the position that the door of hope – the door of opportunity – is to be shut upon any man, no matter how worthy, purely upon the grounds of race or color. Such an attitude would, according to my convictions, be fundamentally wrong." Theodore Roosevelt, 1902

"Our aim is not to do away with corporations; on the contrary, these big aggregations are an inevitable development of modern industrialism. We are not hostile to them; we are merely determined that they shall be so handled as to subserve the public good. We draw the line against misconduct, not against wealth." Theodore Roosevelt, 1902

"The man who is swimming against the stream knows the strength of it." Woodrow Wilson, 1915

"The history of liberty is a history of resistance." Woodrow Wilson, 1916

"Beware of that small group of selfish men who would clip the wings of the American Eagle in order to feather their own nests." Franklin D. Roosevelt, 1936

"So, first of all, let me assert my firm belief that the only thing we have to fear is fear itself – nameless, unreasoning, unjustified terror which paralyzes needed efforts to convert retreat into advance." Franklin D. Roosevelt, 1933

"No matter how long it may take us to overcome this premediated invasion, the American people in their righteous might will win through to absolute victory... With confidence in our armed forces, with the unbounding determination of our people, we will gain the inevitable triumph so help us God." Franklin D. Roosevelt, Dec. 8, 1941, the day after the Japanese attacked Pearl Harbor

"A vital element in keeping the peace is our military establishment. Our arms must be might, ready for instant action, so that no potential aggressor may be tempted to risk his own destruction... This conjunction of an immense military establishment and a large arms industry is new in the American experience... Yet, we must not fail to comprehend its grave implications. In the councils of government, we must guard against the acquisition of unwarranted influence, whether sought or unsought, by the <u>military – industrial complex</u>. The potential for the disastrous rise of misplaced power exists and will persist." Dwight D. Eisenhower's farewell address, 1961

"Ask not what your country can do for you, but what you can do for your country." John F. Kennedy's Inaugural Address, 1961

"For the problems are not all solved and the battles are not all won – and we stand today on the edge of a New Frontier... But the New Frontier of which I speak is not a set of promises – it is a set of challenges. It sums up not what I intend to offer the American people, but what I intend to ask of them." John F. Kennedy's Speech, Democratic National Convention, 1960

"We should live our lives as though Christ was coming this afternoon." Jimmy Carter, 1976

"We must adjust to changing times and still hold to unchanging principles." Jimmy Carter, 1977

"Government's view of the economy could be summed up in a few short phrases: If it moves, tax it. If it keeps moving, regulate it. And if it stops moving, subsidize it." Ronald Reagan, 1986

"If the Soviet Union let another political party come

into existence, they would still be a one-party state, because everybody would join the other party." Ronald Reagan, 1983

"You know, it has been said that politics is the second oldest profession and I've come to realize over the last few years, it bears a great similarity to the first." Ronald Reagan, 1977

"Government is not the solution to our problem; government is the problem." Ronald Reagan's Inaugural Address, 1981

We believe that all of the above great leaders were ten times more in touch with the middle class, average American's needs than our current out of touch politicians, be it Democrat or Republican. Since 2009, they have forgotten all about you because they have been to busy fighting amongst themselves and following the official party line. As Democrats they are required to be Left Wing, Liberal Socialists favoring a big central government. As Republicans they are required to be Right Wing, Conservative, Free Enterprise Advocates favoring a more restricted central government.

Imagine you are a Democrat. You drive your vehicle into a very large field and keep turning left because that is what the Party requires you to do.

Imagine you are a Republican. You drive your vehicle into

a very large field and keep turning right because that is what the Party requires you to do.

What is your route of travel in both cases? A very large circle. What is your final destination in both cases? The same place where you started. How far have you travelled in both cases? You have gone nowhere. Welcome to the Congressional Travel Map – 2009 through 2020. What would George Washington, a former surveyor, have to say about the map to nowhere? I believe he'd say: "I told you so."

Our proposed Party will not have rigid rules as to when we have to turn left or right. Our party will use reason, facts, and common sense to put honest Middle Class Americans in political offices who are responsive to the Middle Class. In the foregoing example of driving into a large field... we would drive straight through it, find the nearest road, find the nearest large highway, and quickly and efficiently reach our intended destination.

So people, maybe it is time for you to grab your mops and your brooms, and mop up the Democrats and sweep out the Republicans. I know you have those cleaning tools handy around your house, because unlike your rich and powerful rulers... you can't afford a maid or butler. And don't worry about your rulers getting upset with you because they don't remember what mops and brooms look like since they have not had to use them for decades.

ABOUT THE AUTHOR

JAMES C. WEART WAS BORN on a Naval Air Station in the United States in February of 1948. His father was a Navy Aviator and his mother was the daughter of an Army Major General. As such, he was raised in a very disciplined military environment wherein duty, honor, country, and self-sacrifice were stressed. The family usually moved from one Navy Base to the next every two to three years causing him to live in Puerto Rico, Virginia, California, Washington State, Maryland, back to Virginia, Rhode Island, Virginia again, and finally Florida where he graduated from Escambia High School at the age of 18. Throughout all the moves as a child he had excelled at sports such as football, wrestling, and baseball, ultimately being named co-captain and best lineman for the Escambia High School football team in 1965.

In July of 1966, he entered his grandfather's alma mater at the United States Military Academy in West Point, New York. He stayed there during Plebe and Yearling years (Freshman and Sophomore) until June of 1968, when he resigned due to philosophical differences with the way the Academy was being run. When training in the field he excelled in marksmanship, hand to hand combat, forced marches, and tactics. However, it appeared to him that the powers at the Academy only cared about "Appearances" such a parades, uniforms, spit shined shoes, polished brass, squared off bed sheets, properly folded socks and underwear, scrubbed floors and toilets, and a lot of cadet brown nosing. He resigned in disgust stating that if they wanted a warrior and leader, they had one, but if they wanted a butler, maid, and shoeshine guy, they had the wrong person. His rebellious spirit and take-charge attitude were not appreciated by the upper classmen who wrote up demerits on a regular basis. He also did not appreciate the fact that he was literally locked up for those two years unable to leave the facility.

After leaving West Point, he enrolled at Stetson University in Deland, Florida, in August of 1968 and entered an ROTC Program. He enjoyed the last two years of college. He graduated in June of 1970 with a Bachelor of Arts in History and Political Science. He was commissioned as a Second Lieutenant in the U.S. Army and assigned to the Engineer Corps because of the math, science, and engineering courses he had taken at West Point. Due to a delayed entry into Army Engineer Officer Basic Course at Fort Belvoir, Virginia, he did not enter active service until January of 1971. He completed the Officer Basic and Advanced Engineer Courses in May of 1971. He was transferred to the 931st Engineer Group at Fort Benning, Georgia, where he became a platoon leader for approximately 42 men. He volunteered for the Vietnam War and received orders to report to Long Bin, South Vietnam, in October of 1971. Unfortunately, for him, President Richard Nixon wanted to win the 1972 presidential election and announced in late August of 1971, "We're going to bring the boys home." Lieutenant Weart's orders to Vietnam were immediately cancelled along with numerous other troops at Fort Benning. He was upset as he had been training for that war for four and one half years. He called the Bureau of Personnel at the Pentagon to protest only to be told by a Major: "Sorry Lieutenant, you have a combat MOS and all combat troops are being recalled as we are turning the war over to the ARVN." Lieutenant Weart replied: "Sir I think that's a big mistake," and as history has shown, he was right. He continued as a platoon leader until January of 1972, when the Brigade Commander transferred new trials, post-conviction relief, appealing improper judicial rulings, setting aside driver license suspensions, suppression of intoxilyzer results, limiting certain statements or admissions of witnesses, limiting police officers opinions, and a myriad of other technical motions. He was a member of the Florida Bar, Georgia Bar and the Federal Middle District of Florida. He has appeared before the 5th District Court of Appeal in Daytona Beach, Florida, The Supreme Court of Florida in Tallahassee and the 11th Circuit of Appeals in Atlanta, Georgia, and had one appeal reach the U.S. Supreme Court. In 2017 and 2018 he was proclaimed one of the ten best criminal lawyers in the State of Florida by several national organizations. One young assistant State Attorney (prosecutor) told him at the time of his retirement that his reputation at the State Attorney's Office was that of a fearless bull dog, who would take a case to trial that no attorney in his right mind would try, and probably win it. They were glad to see him go.

He currently resides in the mountains of Eastern Tennessee with his wife and three dogs, riding his motorcycles through the curvy mountain roads whenever the weather allows.

ACKNOWLEDGEMENT

THE AUTHOR WOULD LIKE TO express his heartfelt appreciation to Marie West and Rebecca Baker for all their hard work in transcribing and correcting this book, and to Greg Hewitt for his unique artwork on the cover of the book.

He would also commend his lovely wife, Corki Weart, for putting up with him while he was working on this book.